THE
GAME

THE
GAME
MICAH RICHARDS
PLAYER. PUNDIT. FAN.

HarperCollins*Publishers*

HarperCollins*Publishers*
1 London Bridge Street
London SE1 9GF

www.harpercollins.co.uk

HarperCollins*Publishers*
Macken House, 39/40 Mayor Street Upper
Dublin 1, D01 C9W8, Ireland

First published by HarperCollins*Publishers* 2022

1 3 5 7 9 10 8 6 4 2

A catalogue record of this book is
available from the British Library

HB ISBN 978-0-00-855288-6
PB ISBN 978-0-00-855289-3

Printed and bound in the UK using 100%
renewable electricity at CPI Group (UK) Ltd

To all those who burst onto the scene

CONTENTS

1

BURSTING ONTO THE SCENE

I felt invincible. I was 18. I'd just made my debut for England. I had my little place in history. I was the youngest defender ever to play for the national team. That night, I'd been up against Arjen Robben, one of the best players of his generation, one of the finest wingers of his time. After the game, he'd talked about how impressed he'd been. This wasn't some nobody. This wasn't a journeyman. This was Arjen Robben. I used to watch him on the television. He'd been impressed. By me.

I was the next big thing at Manchester City. I'd only made a couple of dozen appearances, only been in the first team for a few months, but I was already being treated like a senior player. The fans were convinced that I was the future. I was the golden boy. I could do no wrong. There was a new contract in the works. It would tie me down for five and a half years. It was the longest deal the club had ever offered anyone.

My life had changed beyond recognition. I had an Aston Martin on the driveway. I was using a Range Rover as a runaround. I could afford to buy my own house, to buy my mum's house, and still have money left over for holidays in Los Angeles and Las Vegas and for whatever watch took my fancy. There were agents scrapping over me, promising the world. Pretty soon, I'd be taken down to Coutts, the Queen's bank, and be given the VIP treatment.

More important than that, though, the thing that meant the most, was that I knew I had made it, and that it wasn't going to go away.

There is no such thing as an overnight success in football. Nobody bursts onto the scene, not really. It might have looked from the outside like I'd come from nowhere, but it doesn't work like that. That wasn't the start of my career. Just like everyone else who gets all the way to the Premier League, years of work had gone into that moment. I'd spent hours driving to training, me, my dad and my brother. I'd been enrolled in Manchester City's academy since the age of 14. I'd moved away from home when I wasn't much more than a child. I'd done all of it to chase something I knew, even then, was a one in a million chance. And that might have been being optimistic.

There are a handful of kids who are sure things. They're people like Jermaine Pennant, who signed for Arsenal at 15. Or Wayne Rooney, who was scoring wonder-goals for Everton when he was 16. Or Aaron Lennon, who grew up not too far from me, and James Milner, both of them playing for Leeds at the same age. Leeds were struggling a bit at the time, but the point still stands. Those kids never need to worry.

They're the exceptions. For the rest of us, it doesn't work like that. Even when you have spent your entire life playing, even when you have been at a Premier League academy since you started high school, it's a very fine line. There are too many things that can go wrong. It might be a serious injury, one that stops you playing altogether. Or it might be a minor injury, but one that comes at just the wrong time. It might be that you stop growing, and the club decides you're too small. It might be that you grow too much. It might be a bad decision, or a family member that demands too much, or it might be a coach that just doesn't like you. It might be that, through no fault of your own, some other kid emerges who plays in your position, but does everything quicker and stronger and better than you. There are no guarantees. There is no certainty.

There are always cautionary tales. I still remember the names of a couple. Sam Williamson was with me in City's academy. He'd been there for years. They'd picked him up far earlier than me, in fact. He had plenty of talent. We got to the final of the FA Youth Cup together. But it never really happened for Sam. He only played once for the first team. He ended up playing for Wrexham and for Fleetwood, briefly, and then his career stopped. He did better than millions of people: he was a professional foot-baller. But he didn't make it, not in the way he'd have hoped to make it. He didn't get there and stay there.

Stevie Jordan was older than me; he was part of the first team while I was still at the academy. He played 50 times for City, and then made hundreds of appearances in the Football League. He played for Burnley and for Sheffield

United. He was a footballer for almost 20 years, and he still works in the game now. It's the sort of career that plenty of people dream about. But I don't know if it was the sort of career he thought he'd have, when he was a teenager playing in the Premier League. He made it much further than most. But he didn't quite make it all the way.

I never assumed that I would be any different. I knew how delicate everything was. I knew that being at City's academy didn't mean I would get a professional deal. I knew that getting a professional deal didn't mean I would ever make the first team. I knew that making my debut, playing in the Premier League, sharing a pitch with Thierry Henry, didn't mean I would get a long-term contract. I knew there was a chance, a really good chance, that within a couple of years I'd be playing in League Two or the Conference, trying to start again.

It was only when I had played for England that I knew I had passed the final hurdle. That was the first time I'd ever been sure it wouldn't all end as fast as it had started. I had proved that I could cope with that level. I'd impressed Arjen Robben. I'd trained with Steven Gerrard and Frank Lampard and the rest of the golden generation. I'd proved that I belonged. After that, it couldn't just fade away. I had made it, and I was here to stay. After all that work, after all those milestones, for the very first time I felt like I was now a footballer.

I didn't know what that meant, of course. Not really. If you'd asked me then, I would have said that it meant being an absolute don. It all seemed a bit like a fantasy. You're getting paid a ridiculous amount of money to do something that you love, and you only have to work a couple of hours a day. The papers can't stop talking about how talented you are. The fans are comparing you to anyone and everyone. You feel like a king in your own city. You get the best tables in nightclubs. The champagne bottles suddenly have sparklers in them. You do your shopping at Harvey Nichols and Harrods.

But that, as I learned pretty quickly, is only one side of football. There are others. I wasn't invincible, as it turned out. It isn't all a fantasy. There are times when you dread going into training, because the senior players make those couple of hours feel like a lifetime, or because the manager seems determined to make your life a misery. There are times when you're out of the team, and you can't see a way to get back into it, or when you're picked last for a five-a-side in training and you know, just know, that all of your teammates secretly think you're shit. There are times when the fans are convinced that you're useless, and that makes you think you're useless, and there are times when the club that said it wanted to keep you forever is trying to shift you to whoever it can. Nobody can really prepare you for any of that. They definitely can't prepare you for it if you grew up where I did.

Chapeltown has a certain reputation. In Leeds, it's the bad part of town. People will tell you that the tightly packed streets are full of drugs and gangs, that you can't walk around at night, that it's the sort of place where everyone does what they can to get out. And some of that, unfortunately, is true. We all knew the streets where the dealers did their trade, even if we weren't exactly sure, as kids, what the trade was. The language they used meant nothing to me. Some of the people I grew up with did find themselves sucked into that life. There are a lot of people in Chapeltown who have not been given very many choices.

It would be easy for me to present that picture of my childhood, to go along with the stereotype of Chapeltown, to use it to make me look good. Who doesn't want everyone to think that they're an inspiring rags-to-riches story? But I can't do that, because that reputation isn't the only truth.

I loved growing up in Chapeltown. I loved going to get fish and chips from Cantor's. I loved Maureen's, where the Caribbean food is so good that once, when I was 11 or 12, I saw Rio Ferdinand and Olivier Dacourt dropping in to grab some jerk chicken and fried dumplings. We didn't get many Premier League footballers in Chapeltown. We didn't get many silver Aston Martins parked up on the pavement, either. Most of all, I loved being in a place where people liked the same things as me, where people thought the same way as me and – as football started to take me to parts of the city and the country where I stood out – I loved being in a place where people looked like me.

Maybe I can only say that because I was luckier than a lot of people. My mum was (and still is) a diamond. We didn't have a lot of money and we didn't have a lot of things, but she gave us the best upbringing she could manage. She gave all of us the right values, the right attitudes. Though my parents weren't together, my dad was around. He has always been a massive presence in my life. He worked every hour he could find so that he could drive me to training. A lot of people I knew didn't have that kind of support.

I wasn't naive, of course. I knew there were places and people to avoid. Mostly, that wasn't difficult. Their world, that world, had nothing to do with me. Only occasionally did I catch a glimpse of it. I saw some things I would rather not have seen. But that Chapeltown wasn't my Chapeltown. Sadly, the police didn't quite understand that. You grow up as a black kid in a place like Chapeltown and you get used to being stopped by the police. You get used to hearing them call you a black bastard. You get used to them using the n-word. It makes you angry. It makes you scared. It happens now, when I go back. I lose count of the number of times I've been pulled over, always with the same excuse: a car matching this description has been reported for something or other. I always give the same answer. If I was a drug dealer, would I really be driving round a place like Chapeltown in a Lamborghini, drawing attention to myself? No, I wouldn't. So stop lying to me, or even better, stop randomly pulling people over because they're black.

There is a reason, though, that I have always gone back. My career has taken me to Oldham, to Manchester, to Florence and to Birmingham. It's allowed me to live in the countryside, to go on holiday to Los Angeles and Las Vegas. But no matter where I went or what I did, Chapeltown was never just the place where I grew up. It wasn't simply where I used to live. It was home. It still is.

That was never something I struggled to remember, even as my life changed beyond recognition. Nobody can warn you in advance about what being a footballer is actually like, how intense it can be, how much your world shifts, how weird it can be, how much it makes you feel like you're no longer on the same planet as the one you used to know. Most of the time, you have to work it out by yourself. Most of the time, all you can do is make it up as you go along.

In the end, my career was quite a short one. I made my debut for England, cleared that last barrier, in 2006. I played my last game of any kind ten years later. It won't surprise anyone to learn that I came off injured after about an hour. I was only 28. I hung around for a little while longer – I had a contract to see out – but my time as a footballer, really, only lasted a decade. Just as quickly as I'd burst onto the scene, I burst off it, too.

But in that time, I like to think that I packed plenty in. I won the FA Cup. I won the Premier League title, twice, though in truth I didn't contribute much to one of them. I played for England. I played for Great Britain, too, which is not something many people in my line of work can say. I saw the club I played for bought out and taken over three times, one of them not completely disastrously. I had the fun of being young and reckless, and the responsibility of being old and experienced, and worked out fast that I much preferred one to the other.

I worked under some of the finest minds of their generation, as well as Rémi Garde. I was scouted by Manchester United and Chelsea and Real Madrid, and I was also offered on a cut-price deal to Wigan Athletic. I played alongside Robbie Fowler and David Beckham, Sergio Agüero and Yaya Touré. I told Robinho where to get his hair cut. I vandalised Vincent Kompany's locker, but I should point out that he deserved it. I shinned down a fire escape with David Silva and went out for long lunches with Mohamed Salah. I fell out with coaches and agents. I swore at Garth Crooks live on the BBC, although not on purpose, and I haven't done it again. I turned down contracts on a whim and met managers, secretly, in hotel rooms to try to organise a transfer. I opened the door to my house one night to find Mario Balotelli standing there with a load of fireworks, a fuse, and a smile on his face. I had a long-running argument about a fence with Nigel de Jong. And then, when I retired, I managed to make Roy Keane smile.

Through all of that, I got a pretty good view of what football is like. I saw every side it can offer: the glorious ones and the ugly ones, the happy ones and the sad ones, the successes and the failures. I saw how fun it can be and how brutal it can be and how weird it can be, especially if your club decides to spend tens of millions of pounds on Mario Balotelli and for some reason puts you in charge of his behaviour.

I did not, as it turned out, have the career I thought I would. Maybe nobody does. I didn't think it would be so brief. I didn't think it would end so abruptly. I didn't think it would leave me as low as I have ever been. But I also didn't think it would take me abroad, or bring me a Premier League winner's medal, or involve Tim Sherwood telling me at great length that he thought I was rubbish, but that he wanted me to be his captain anyway.

The game isn't what it seems from the outside. The game isn't quite what I was expecting, when I first broke through, when I thought I was invincible. The game doesn't always work like the people on television think it does. The game is better, worse and stranger than you can imagine, and that is coming from someone who saw it all with their own eyes.

2

THE DRESSING-ROOM PYRAMID

Every manager does it. They think it's fun. A little treat, a bit of a gift. A light-hearted five-a-side competition to end a training session. It's supposed to be a chance for the squad to forget all of the pressure that comes with being a professional and remember what it was like when you played football as a kid. And it can be, as long as they avoid the single worst thing any manager can do. You should never, ever, ask your players to pick teams.

You know the drill. It's the same as you would get in a PE lesson at school. Four people are chosen as captains. Generally, that will be four of the most senior players. At Manchester City, that might have been Vincent Kompany, Joleon Lescott, Gaël Clichy and me, say. The goalkeepers are excluded: they'll rotate, keep things fair. Then, one by one, the captains will choose. Kompany might pick Yaya Touré. Lescott would go for David Silva. I'd have Sergio Agüero. That means Clichy choosing Carlos Tevez. Then we would go round again, all the way through a squad of

20 or so extremely talented, extremely competitive footballers, until you have four teams.

It's not hard to guess the problem. Someone has to be
chosen last. Until that point, you've spent your entire life
as the best player on any team you joined. You were better
than all of your mates at school. You got picked up by an
academy, and you shone there. The coaches marked you
out for greatness. By the time you were a teenager, agents
were fighting over you. The big sportswear brands, Nike
and Adidas and Puma, started to offer you free boots and
maybe, after a while, a juicy contract to wear their stuff.
You signed professional terms. You joined the first team,
made your debut. People started to recognise you in the
street. You got tables in all the best clubs. You bought a
Bentley or a souped-up Range Rover or an Audi R8. You
were going to be a star. You were a star. You got your
multi-million-pound transfer to one of the biggest clubs in
the world. You're Premier League. You're Champions
League. You've made it.

And now here you are, watching as everyone else gets
chosen, and you're still standing there like a plum. Wayne
Bridge? He's gone. James Milner? Him too. Then it's
Matija Nastasić, someone who never broke through at
City but a demon at five-a-side. You can see people shrink-
ing at this point, full of fear that they aren't going to hear
their name, that nobody is going to choose them. These
mammoths start to become frightened little mice. Then,
after everyone else is gone, it's just you, the wooden spoon,
the runt of the litter, being told in no uncertain terms by all
of your teammates that they think you are a bit, well, crap.

It is the most embarrassing thing that can happen to you as a footballer, and it is devastating. I know it's devastating not just because I saw good players, people like Javi García and Stefan Savić – players who graced the knock-out stages of the Champions League – distraught at being picked last, but because it happened to me. Almost, anyway. Not at Manchester City, admittedly. I was safe there, because I always made sure I was a captain. But towards the end of my career, at Aston Villa, I was picked second to last. There wasn't even the saving grace of being in a squad packed with the best players on the planet. I'd played for England at 18 and here I was, being picked behind Ritchie De Laet. There were academy kids going before me. I was picked 19th out of 20. That is bad, and it was incredibly difficult to deal with. I used to be the star of the show. I was the main event, the central character, and now I'm all the way down here. My head went completely. It was so humiliating that, as soon as it happened, my first thought was that I had to retire.

That's not the only problem with asking players to pick sides. A dressing room is a fragile creature. You're all part of a team, obviously. You're all pulling in the same direction, striving for the same goal, trying to achieve the same things. You know, of course, that you need your teammates if you're going to achieve all of the things that you want to achieve: to win that title, to play in the Champions League, to avoid relegation, whatever it might be. But you have your own individual ambitions, too: you want to win the league, but you don't want to be a substitute. You want to be playing. You don't want someone else taking your place. You might be teammates. You might even be friends. You want them to do well. But you definitely do not want them to do better than you. You're a team, but you're not. It's ruthless and it's cut-throat, and in that sort of environment you tend to huddle together for protection.

Every dressing room in football is divided into different tribes, little factions and cliques. A lot of the time, in an era when every Premier League team has a patchwork of players from all over the world, there's an assumption that it breaks down according to language. That's true to an extent: players will obviously hit it off much more quickly and much more easily with people they can communicate with. You might have a little enclave of Spanish and Portuguese speakers, a group that clusters around the French contingent, and then a core of English or British players. Certainly, in the year that I spent at Fiorentina, that was what happened to me: my Italian never stretched much beyond saying 'Bravo' very loudly whenever there was a lull in conversation, so I attached myself to the half a dozen members of the squad who spoke English.

But language isn't the most important factor. It can help you make friends, help you find your gang, but it doesn't define where you belong. Instead, everything in the hierarchy of a dressing room is arranged according to ability.

At the top of the pile, you have the best player. The rest of the squad will know full well who the best player is, even if they don't particularly want to admit it. Most of the time, the best player will also be what we used to call 'HP': highest paid. When you're HP, when you're the top dog, you can basically do what you want. You're the one who decides the mood of the dressing room. You're untouchable, and everyone else's job is to feed your ego.

That honour, at Manchester City, fell to Yaya Touré. We had some incredibly talented footballers while I was there, people like Tevez and Agüero and David Silva, but Yaya was something else. Yaya was the one who made things happen. Even Roberto Mancini recognised that. In the year we won the club's first title in almost half a century, we lost a game at Everton not long after Christmas. Yaya was missing that day, away on international duty at the Africa Cup of Nations, and we deserved to lose. Mancini pulled us into the dressing room after the game and told us, in no uncertain terms, that we were 'shit without Yaya'. If we were going to win the league, he said, we couldn't be so reliant on him.

It was a message to us, of course, a way of challenging everyone else to prove that we could be just as good without Yaya as we were when he was in the team; an attempt to make sure that he got a reaction from us for the rest of the season. But it was also a message to Yaya. Mancini was brilliant at that. He knew just how to make him feel special; he'd been the best player at Lazio and Sampdoria, too, so I suppose he knew what was needed. He would never blame him, never criticise him, never do anything that might annoy him. Mancini was well aware that we weren't a one-man team – he delivered that speech with David Silva and Sergio Agüero sitting right there – but he needed to make Yaya think we were. That was what it took to get the best out of him.

The most pervasive myth in football is that all players need to be treated equally. There has to be a defined set of rules, obviously, ones that everyone has to accept and follow, but you can't treat someone like Mario Balotelli the same way you treat someone like James Milner. And you always have to make an exception for your star: not just the manager, but the players, too.

It's nonsense when people say that Cristiano Ronaldo's or Mohamed Salah's teammates won't forgive them for failing to put in the hard yards, to track back, to follow their runners, to help out defensively. Of course they will. They'll not only forgive them, they'll do all of that work for them happily. You'll accommodate your best player. You'll shift around for them. You'll do their running for them. You'll recognise that that isn't their game. You'll do all the dirty work on their behalf, and you'll do it with a smile on your face and a song in your heart, just so long as they keep up their end of the bargain and win games for you. If they do that, you'll forgive your best player almost anything.

It's only when they don't that you have a problem. Yaya wasn't cold, not really, but he could be a little distant. He put up barriers. It took him a while to trust people, I think, which is natural when you think about what he represents in the Ivory Coast: together with Didier Drogba, he's the biggest star the country has ever produced. He's a hero. He's an icon. He was used to being treated as such.

I handled him a bit differently. I was confident that nobody could ever accuse me of shirking. I might not have been as talented as him, but I worked as hard as anyone, and I stood up for what was best for the team. I was always happy to make clear that I'd do whatever I could for him, just so long as he made sure he delivered. If he thought he could phone it in, if he thought he could do what he wanted, then I'd challenge him. That's the bargain. You need the star player to try so that you can win games. But they need you, too, to run that little bit more for them. If they stop trying, they're taking the piss out of you. And most players don't like having the piss taken out of them.

As for everyone else, they have to find their place below the top of the pyramid. First, though, they have to establish whether they will be accepted at all.

First impressions matter in football. Players are naturally quite wary. When you sign for a new club, the squad might be welcoming. Your new teammates will be friendly enough. They're waiting, though, to find out how good you are. They won't come to you. They need to see what you've got. And they need to see it quickly.

The first rondo of the first training session sets the tone. That's when everyone is watching to see what they're dealing with: whether your touch is up to it, whether you can live with the level. The higher up you go, the more demanding that becomes. Players who shine for mid-table teams can't always survive when they move to a side trying to win the title or compete in the Champions League. There's no such thing as a bad professional player, not really; there's definitely no such thing as a bad Premier League player. But there are players who look bad in the context, who aren't up to the required standard, and your teammates will make that judgement extremely quickly.

In a really tough club, the rest of the squad will have decided what they make of you by the end of that first day. You might, if you're lucky, get two. Kinder souls might even allow a new player a whole pre-season to bed in. But that's the absolute maximum. If you haven't proved that you can live with the level by then, you're cooked. You might have been signed for millions of pounds, but you're immediately dismissed as one of the misfits and the outcasts. You can go and stand over there.

If you're deemed good enough, then you can start to work out where you fit in. Every squad is different, of course, and every dressing room has its own unique blend of personalities. As a rule, the higher up you go, the bigger and more pronounced those personalities are. Big players tend to be big characters. They all, though, fit in to one of a handful of moulds, ones that are immediately recognisable to anyone who has been in a dressing room.

It's probably easiest to think of a dressing room as being a bit like school, except that everyone involved is in theory a grown-up, and they also drive extremely expensive cars. The best players are the cool kids: everyone wants to be mates with them. Around them are a group of hangers-on. Now sometimes, those hangers-on are good enough to count as cool kids themselves, but sometimes they're not. Sometimes it's incredibly obvious that they are just trying to bask in the reflected glory of the best player. It happens all the time: when Cristiano Ronaldo first started to take the Premier League by storm, a little clique grew around him at Manchester United. Those players were talented, obviously. They were internationals. They won the

Premier League title. But they weren't really good enough to run with him. They weren't at his level. They were clinging on to him for protection. They wanted to be as close as possible to him so that their position was secure. They were barnacles, and everyone knew exactly what they were doing. It would be like me claiming to be best mates with Sergio Agüero. Nobody would buy it.

The first group in any dressing room stands a little apart from all of that. They're the dads. There are always a couple of dads. They're the really experienced players, the ones who have been around for a while. They might be coming to the end of their careers, or certainly at the peak of them. They're sure of their places. They take responsibility. They're the elder statesmen. Richard Dunne, when I first started at Manchester City, was a dad.

He tends to be forgotten a little, given everything that happened to City in the years after he left, but he qualifies as one of the club's greatest ever players. He was player of the year four years in a row. He barely ever missed a game, and if he did you knew it was because he was genuinely injured: Richard Dunne would make it through anything short of a detached limb. He was quick enough, and strong as a bull. He set the tone and the culture. He might not have quite warranted a statue outside the Etihad Stadium, but that he's overlooked is just an accident of birth, really. He was at the club just a little too early. He was there at just the wrong time.

He made playing alongside him so easy. He would talk me through games. He taught me how to play central defence at a time when I was still learning the position.

That was how he was with quite a lot of the younger players. He had a real paternal streak.

That, really, is what the dressing-room dads do. They look after the second group: the kids. They're usually the young bucks, the hopefuls just coming through. Sometimes, they've come from the academy. That's not an easy step to make. You're there to take someone's job, after all, and there's a lot of senior players who do not take to that well. They make your life as difficult as possible. You need the dads to guide you, to help you, to make sure you feel as comfortable as you can in that first-team environment.

But not all kids are young. Some players are kids, no matter where they've come from or how much they've cost or how many games they've played. It's an extreme example, but Mario Balotelli was the definition of a kid. People have the wrong impression of Mario. We spent a lot of time together when he was at Manchester City. We clicked: we were the same age, we had similar interests, we shared a sense of humour. I loved the fact that, despite the fact he attracted more attention than anyone I played with other than David Beckham, he was just unapologetically himself. He was authentic. He was real. I've always tried to be that way, too. We were so close that people used to call us twins, though probably not identical ones, because I was better looking.

But it is true to say that Mario needed to be indulged and understood and, just occasionally, steered in a certain direction. Mario got away with murder under Mancini because he knew he was talented enough to score a couple of goals in a derby or produce the assist – the only time he set up a goal in the Premier League for Manchester City – for Sergio Agüero to win the league. If a kid is talented enough, that's the sort of treatment they'll get. Up to a certain point, anyway. After a while, no matter how good they are, you can't help them if they just keep setting a load of fireworks off in their own house. There are limits, even in football.

Then there are the politicians: the sly ones, the crafty ones, the ones who always have just a little bit of an agenda. They're the ones you have to watch. Sometimes, their motives are pretty obvious. When I first came through at City, there was a spell when the papers were linking me with all of the big clubs. Arsenal were in for me. Chelsea were in for me. Manchester United and Liverpool were in for me. This was at a time when City's aims were not quite as grand as they are now, and as a rule most of the squad were really pleased for me. They were happy to think that I might get a big move. Or maybe they were happy to think that I might leave. It's hard to be sure.

Word got back to me, though, that there was one member of the squad who was less than convinced. Apparently, you could find hundreds of right-backs in France who could do exactly what I could do, and for a quarter of the cost. There was no way, by all accounts, that anyone should be thinking of paying £20 million for me. It shouldn't really be a surprise that the person talking me down was a rival for my position. That's what I mean: you're a team, but you're not. All footballers have to balance the needs of the club with their own personal ambitions.

If they're politicians by circumstance, then there are others who are politicians by inclination. They always have something going on, even if it's not really clear why. At one point, we had an attempted coup at Manchester City: we found out that one player had been lobbying other members of the squad to try to persuade them that Vincent Kompany shouldn't be captain anymore. He wanted a few of the more high-profile players to go to the manager and demand a change of regime. It didn't work – as much as Kompany wasn't everyone's cup of tea, everyone respected him – but it upset another faction in the dressing room: the chameleons.

They tend to be warm, genuine, lovely, the backbone of the squad. Sometimes, they might be dads, but sometimes they might be kids, too, depending on what sort of mood they're in. They can switch between groups. They might speak a couple of different languages: Gaël Clichy was a prime example of a chameleon. He spoke English, French and Spanish, so he could be mates with most of the squad. It's the chameleons that bind everyone together. They're not really bothered by the politics of it, and they don't care a huge amount about what everyone else thinks about them.

You need the chameleons to help control another faction within a squad: the firebrands. You encounter more and more of these as the level increases. Craig Bellamy was a firebrand; he was such a firebrand that he was the only person who ever made Gareth Barry, a prime example of a chameleon, lose his temper. It was, I think, Bellamy's first training session with City. He'd already chewed up and spat out Richard Dunne for making a mistake. 'No wonder we're always losing, if you're the captain!' he shouted. You can't talk to the captain of the club like that. Craig didn't let that stop him. A few minutes later, Barry didn't pass him the ball during a training game. He started ranting at him: you give me the ball when I tell you to give me the ball, you fucking this and that. Gareth Barry was as calm as they come, but he just lost it. They squared up to each other. Like good teammates, we all stopped to watch, urging Barry to hit him. That was Bellamy, though. He could be personal – he could be vicious – but it was because he had standards and he wanted to maintain them. We got used to him. Eventually.

Samir Nasri, too, was a big character. The best way to sum up Samir Nasri is to say that you'd really want him on your team, largely so that you didn't have to face him. I've never met a man so dedicated to arguing with everyone, all of the time. I liked him for that. My mentality was similar. I would never let anyone have a go at me. That's not always the ideal mix, of course: there was one game, at home against Norwich, where we managed to talk ourselves to the very edge of having a fight on the pitch. I can't really remember what it was about – I'm sure he was wrong, though – but all of a sudden, with 50,000 people inside the Etihad watching, we were walking towards each other, shouting and bawling and nobody backing down. At some point, we must both have remembered what we were doing and where we were and left it, but it was a close-run thing. There was a point where I would happily have punched him. You need people like him, and Bellamy, though. Players have to challenge each other, to hold each other to account. That's the only way a team gets better.

But just as important are people who can break that tension, and that is why jokers are crucial. Every squad needs a couple of jokers, too. I was a joker. I never minded that tag: I was confident enough that people could have a laugh at my expense without thinking less of me as a player. It is a bit of a sliding scale, though. Aleksandar Kolarov might not look it – he looks like he's about to tell you that your position has been terminated, effective immediately, and that HR will be in touch about your redundancy package – but he was a joker. He loved telling jokes. He had a surprisingly British sense of humour, given that he was Serbian. James Milner always had a reputation for being boring, drinking Ribena and eating digestive biscuits, but he was hilarious, too. Again, you wouldn't really know it to look at him. Or hear him speak. And then, at the extreme end of the scale, was Balotelli. He had a habit of taking things too far. He didn't know when to stop. He was a loose cannon: less of a joker, and more like the Joker.

The thing about all of these categories, though, is that you can move between them. A kid can become a dad as they get older and wiser and stop setting fireworks off in their house. A joker like me can, in the right circumstances, become a politician. The year that Manchester City won that first title, I started off as the first-choice right-back. I'd played in the FA Cup final the year before, and it was my position to lose. And then I go and do my knee. Pablo Zabaleta steps up, takes my place, plays brilliantly. Through no fault of my own, even when I'm fit, I'm second choice. I'm on the bench. All of a sudden, I feel like a different person. Instead of being the funny one, the smiling Micah that everyone knows and mostly tolerates, I'm the sly one. I'm sidling up to people and telling them that all Zabaleta does is smash into people. I'm whispering into other players' ears that, when you stop and think about it, he's actually really slow, and probably shouldn't be in the team, and maybe they should sell him, he'd do quite well for Sunderland. I've become something I don't want to be, something that I would hate in another player. Suddenly, I'm the snake.

There are, occasionally, players who don't fit into any of those groups. Sometimes, that's because they're quiet, peaceful souls, happy to do their own thing. Agüero was a bit like that. It's a strange phrase, the sort you generally only hear when people are accused of crimes, but Sergio tended to keep himself to himself. He wouldn't really come on nights out: he preferred to stay at home and play Xbox. Now it's not for me to say what he should and shouldn't do, and obviously just how famous he was made it difficult for him to live his life as normal, but still: that strikes me as a real waste of being Sergio Agüero.

And sometimes, it's because they're the strongest people in all of football. It might be the best player at a club who defines how a dressing room feels – when they're happy, everyone is happy; when they're moody, everyone is moody – but it is the member of the squad who is most easily overlooked who holds everything together. The most overlooked position in football is, without question, the third-choice goalkeeper.

Playing that role is the most difficult thing I can imagine. You have spent your entire career being a star. You've been a winner at every level: at school and for your junior teams, in the academy, probably for a Championship team, at the very least. You've probably played in the Premier League, or in the top flight in France or Germany or Spain. You would, at one point, have maybe had ambitions to play international football. And now your job is, literally, to turn up and not play football. You work Monday to Friday. Your only job on the weekend is to let player shoot at you in the warm-up. Only if two other people get injured will you actually get the chance to play.

That must take so much mental strength that I cannot begin to imagine it. You're not quite there to make up the numbers, but you're basically employed to be ready not to play. To keep that job, you have to do nothing at all to disturb the peace. You have to keep everyone onside. You have to be popular. You have to be calm and patient and understanding. You can't be upsetting the apple cart, creating problems, moaning and complaining about how the number one is dodgy on crosses or the number two has poor personal hygiene. We had them at Manchester City: Stuart Taylor, Richard Wright and then, after I left, Scott Carson. Nobody ever thinks about them, but they're incredibly important to maintaining the one thing any team needs if it is going to succeed: balance.

That is why asking players to pick teams is such a bad idea. It might not be as much of a laugh, a generous little reminder of what it was like when you were at school, but it is so much easier when the manager does it. They have all sorts of ways of splitting the squad up, some of them more socially acceptable than others. We would play English against foreign, young against old. I had one manager who had absolutely no problem with deciding, quite often, that it was a great day to have the black players on one team and the white lads on another.

Asking the players to do it, though, is a recipe for disaster. It exposes, in just a couple of minutes, all of the fault lines that run underneath a dressing room. Players pick their friends, their mates, the members of their little clan. You need a team to be united. You need everyone to forget that they all have their own ambitions and their own dreams and to believe that they are all part of one team, one big happy family. You do not need to highlight just how many divides there are, or just how fragile the peace that holds everyone together is, no matter how much fun you think it might be.

3

GUCCI SATCHELS FILLED WITH KETCHUP

Vincent Kompany's locker was immaculate. He organised it just as he wanted it. Everything was in the right place: the textbooks for the Masters degree he was doing in Business Studies in one spot, his notes and his coursework in another. That's not what we were looking for, though. All we wanted was one specific folder: the one that contained the fine sheet.

Kompany was Manchester City's prefect. He had been since the moment he arrived. He'd signed a few weeks before the takeover, when the club was owned by Thaksin Shinawatra, after impressing against us in a pre-season friendly, but not as a central defender. He was coming back from an injury, so he played as a central midfielder that day. Not just a central midfielder, actually. He was a playmaker. A number 10. There was this massive guy, with these huge feet, doing delicate skills in the middle of the park, all these little flicks and dragbacks. It would have looked ridiculous if he hadn't been quite good at them. The club paid Hamburg £7 million for him straightaway.

He was never going to be the next Maradona, but he did have a reputation for being able to play in a couple of positions. He'd played in midfield for Anderlecht, the club where he started, and he'd slotted in at centre-back, too. That didn't last long, though. In his first season at City, in an away game against Arsenal, Mark Hughes decided to play him in midfield. He'd go on to play more than 300 times for Manchester City, and I'm pretty confident he never played worse than he did that day. He had an absolute stinker. He could barely control the ball. In fairness to him, he was struggling with a toe injury. He'd had to cut a hole in his sock to let it move around, and every time he touched the ball, he winced with pain. Still, he was bad enough that it kind of put an end to the idea that he could be a utility man. The view in the dressing room was very much that Vincent Kompany was not a central midfielder. He was moved back into defence. Things worked out pretty well for him there: he was strong, aggressive, he could play out, he never let his performances drop.

What made Kompany stand out, though, was his sense of responsibility. Kompany took his job seriously. As captain, he saw himself as the adult in the room. It was up to him to maintain standards, to keep everyone in line. It was also up to him to enforce the rules.

Every dressing room is governed by rules. Every player might need to be handled differently – some need a carrot, some a great big stick – but there is always a set of guidelines that apply equally to everyone. The first one, the most important one, is simple. Don't be late.

For all their flaws, you'll never meet a more punctual group of people than footballers. Footballers have it drummed in to them from a young age that there is no greater crime than turning up late. It's a matter of showing respect to your teammates, to your manager. Fail to prepare, prepare to fail, as the saying goes. I don't remember being especially worried by being late when I was at school: if I arrived for a lesson at ten past nine, I arrived for a lesson at ten past nine. It was no big deal. Football changed that. Football gave me punctuality.

It's stayed with me. Being late, even worrying that I might be late, stresses me out more than almost anything else. I can't take people who are late seriously. Not without an excuse, and a genuine one at that. There was traffic on the way? That depends where you're coming from. If it's a long journey, then maybe. If it's a short one, then you should have taken that into account. Check Google Maps. Make sure you set off in plenty of time. If your train is delayed, that's no problem. That happens. Nothing you can do. Can't be helped. Oh, we were meant to meet at 12 and your train was only scheduled to get in at 11.55? That's different. That's late. You've got to plan for these things happening. My guess is that most players are the same, no matter where they've played or which managers they've had. Everyone accepts that being late, especially for training, is the ultimate taboo. If the manager and their coaches have set up a specific session, it's disrespectful and it's unprofessional to roll up five minutes into it. It's rule number one, across football. Don't be late.

The other rules depend a little more on who your manager might be. Different coaches have different ideas of what is acceptable and what is not. Most of the time, players will be told they are not allowed to go for a night out 48 hours before a game. On away trips, you might not be allowed out of your rooms after 11 p.m. Those are pretty standard. Others change every year. When I first started playing, players would sit around before training reading the newspapers or messing about on their phones. Then, one year, a command came down from on high that there would be no more newspapers in the dressing room. That was a real blow for Stephen Ireland, who couldn't start his morning without flicking through the *Financial Times*. Phones were even more controversial. Some managers ban them in the dressing room: that's a time when you should be talking to your teammates, thinking about the session ahead, not taking a BuzzFeed quiz to find out what character from *Friends* you are, or checking who's in your DMs. Mark Hughes went one step further and banned phones from the building at Manchester City's old training ground at Carrington completely. We had to leave them in the car. That one was a bit much for me. Leave it in the car? What are you supposed to do if there's an emergency at home? I think that one might have fallen by the wayside a bit now: judging by how many players post on social media from the dressing room, there can't be many where phones are banned outright these days.

There are always rules around food, too. They're not quite as severe as people think they'll be. Inside the training ground, everything will be monitored to make sure it's suitable for athletes to eat. The meals on offer in the canteen will be designed to offer the right mix of protein and carbohydrate and fat, but only the good sorts of fats, not the bad sorts. Outside, it used to be a little less regulated. You could eat what you wanted, more or less. There was a Chinese takeaway in Hale, in south Manchester, that I used to go to three times a week. It never occurred to me that certain things should have been off the menu. I was young. My metabolism was good. I'd burn thousands of calories in training every day. I could afford to have a few chicken wings.

That has changed now. A lot of elite players have their own personal chefs now, preparing meals specifically designed for them. Some clubs will send their squad home with meals, too, or even teach them and their partners how to cook the best kind of food. That's no surprise: football has grown more and more body-conscious over the last 20 or 30 years. You can see that from how ripped the players are. They didn't look like that with their shirts off in the 1980s.

I saw that change first-hand. The day that players used to dread more than any other was Body Fat Day. A few times a year, a doctor would turn up at the training ground with nothing more than a notebook and a pair of callipers. Their job was to measure your body fat: pinching an inch on your arm, your back, your leg and your hip, and seeing how much of you was muscle, and how much of you was flab. An amazing score would be under 20 per cent. Between 20 and 30 was fine. Beyond 30 and maybe you had a little bit of a problem. Over 40 and you had to wonder if maybe you'd been hitting those chicken wings a bit too hard.

I should stress that mine was always fine. I was always towards the top of the list. So was Daniel Sturridge. I knew that because the club would put everyone's results on a board, so that we could all see. I think it's what might now be called body-shaming. Nobody wanted to be at the bottom of that list. It could be unbearable if you came last, no matter how good a player you were. Being told you're the fattest at the club: that's not going to work out well for anyone.

Those players who struggled more than most, then, did everything they could to make sure they weren't the wooden spoon. They'd tense their arms so that the doctor couldn't get an accurate measurement. They'd calmly and patiently suggest that he might like to apply a little less pressure with the callipers, so they got a more forgiving reading. They'd tell them to stop almost immediately after starting, so the score was the sort of thing they found acceptable. They'd breezily explain that if they saw their name at the foot of the pile then the doctor might find themselves seeking employment elsewhere. You could tell who'd intimidated the doctor the least by who came bottom. We had some heavy players in those early years at Manchester City. They all seemed to do surprisingly well. It must have mostly been muscle.

When Roberto Mancini came in, he effectively made every day Body Fat Day. It was no longer enough to check what sort of shape we were in every so often; managers now want to keep track all the time. He'd make us get on the scales every morning and make sure that we were the same weight as we had been the previous day. In a lot of ways, he was quite relaxed. He didn't mind the players going out and enjoying themselves. But he didn't want any of us getting away from our fighting weights, and that was how he policed it. Manuel Pellegrini was just as obsessed. During one pre-season, he walked past me, stopped, and then pulled at a little bit of fat on my hip. 'You have to stop eating, huh?' he said. He had a smile on his face, as though he was joking, but he wasn't. I'd been running around all day, burning calories, but he'd obviously decided I wasn't quite as in shape as he wanted. I could tell he was serious because he repeated it. 'Stop eating.' He walked off, shaking his head.

In an industry so concerned with what the players weigh and what they look like, it's probably not a shock that the rules apply even to the most minor things. There is a surprising amount of ketchup politics in football, for example. Fabio Capello, when he was England manager, banned it. He never really gave a reason: he just insisted it wasn't good for us. That's probably right, but at the same time, ketchup is hardly the worst thing in the world. You're an athlete. You're burning thousands of calories in every training session. You can probably handle a little bit of red sauce. Other managers are a little more relaxed about condiments; you quite often find that when the previous manager has had strict rules around food, their replacement will lift them, and the ketchup will come flooding back. It's not really about the ketchup, though.

It's about showing the players that you trust them, and that you're different to your predecessor.

Besides, it's all a little bit pointless. If players want ketchup, they're going to have ketchup. Mancini got rid of condiments, too, but I think less because he was worried about the nutrition and more because he thought it was ruining our food. You never see a bottle of red sauce on the table at a trattoria in some Tuscan square. They don't need it. The food is perfectly seasoned. That was Mancini's approach. He thought we were barbarians for dousing our chef-prepared meals in ketchup. But even that wouldn't stop us. We used to stay at the Radisson in Manchester before home games. We'd wait until Mancini had gone, or wasn't paying attention, and then we'd get the chef over and tell him to go and get the ketchup. I always felt sorry for him. You train your whole life to know how to plate up a high-quality meal. You get a job in the Radisson, so you must be pretty good. You're using only the best ingredients. All of the flavours are perfectly balanced. And then a load of footballers come along and tell you that what it really needs is a big dollop of ketchup.

For away trips, some players would go a step further, and take their own secret supply. That's what all of those Louis Vuitton and Gucci satchels that players carry are for. People think they're full of shampoo and conditioner and expensive aftershaves. They're not. There's nothing in there except a single, precious, bottle of Heinz. It's the same with takeaways. Obviously, when you're in a hotel room before an away game, you're not meant to get a Deliveroo. The club will have a nutritionist who makes sure that everything you put in your body is high-quality, easily digested, unlikely to affect performance. But sometimes it's late at night and you want some chicken. A little bit of midnight chicken can't do anyone any harm, not really. And on those occasions, the way you get that chicken is you find a friendly physio, barge into his room, and order the takeaway there. It's a victimless crime.

Occasionally, the punishments for breaking these rules can be severe. There have been times when team buses have left for games without players because they were late. Mikel Arteta stripped Pierre-Emerick Aubameyang of the Arsenal captaincy because he was late. A few weeks later, he shipped him off to Barcelona. They're the outliers, though. Most of the time, the way the rules are enforced is by a fine system.

What sort of offences lead to a fine – and how high those fines are – depend on the manager and the club, but every team has a fine system. The amount you have to pay has gone up in line with players' wages. A first offence might cost you £500. A second might be a grand. By the time you get to the third, it starts to look like you might have a bit of a problem, so you need a bit of a short, sharp shock. That one might be £5,000. Some transgressions are worse than others. I was never fined for being late – I am, as I said, a very punctual person – but I had a bit of a habit of being fined for fighting in training. Well, I say fighting. They were really more like scuffles. I'd have a scuffle if I'd lost a training game, or if someone had tackled me in a way that I didn't really like.

But the punishment for that was not nearly as severe as the one for skiving. If a player had gone out the previous night and woken up with a bit of a headache, they might call the medical team and plead illness; they'd ask the doctor if maybe they could just let the manager know that they might not be in today. There were times when so many players did it that it was a bit of a problem, and so the managers started to come down hard on it. Being caught trying to skip a session could be a very expensive business.

The managers might set the rules, but it's up to the players to enforce them. That's where Kompany came in. Nobody had a problem with the fact that it was his job to track the fines. It was more that he seemed to enjoy it just a little bit too much. Maybe he wasn't a prefect. He might have been a teacher. A stern headmaster. He was so organised. Every time a player was late or didn't put his bib in the washing basket after training, he'd log it on his little fine sheet, alongside how much every player owed, how many times they'd committed each offence. Then he would store it, very carefully, in his locker.

As one of his vice-captains, he tried to rope me in as his muscle. He wanted me to be the bad cop. It wasn't just that he wanted me to be his snitch, to let him know if I'd spotted any of the rest of the squad breaking the rules, it was that he asked me to be the one who had to go and tell the players they'd been fined, and get them to cough up the money.

I didn't have a problem with the system. There have to be rules in a dressing room. I might have had a fair few mishaps – that's a good word for them – in my career, but I'm pretty sure none of my managers would have a bad word to say about my professionalism. I worked hard. I did my bit. Fine, I might have had a couple of scraps in training and there may have been times when I didn't strictly adhere to curfews, but I was never late.

It's not that Kompany's iron rule wasn't just. There was an appeals system: you had to go with him to the manager's office and plead your case. Only once the ultimate authority had decided you were guilty did you have to sign a disclaimer saying the money could be deducted from your wages and directed, instead, to the club's fine jar. At the end of the year, all of that money would be counted and divided: some of it would go to the Christmas party, some of it would go to charity, and some of it would go to the rest of the staff at the club, the people who worked on reception and made the food and cleaned the kit and generally made our lives ridiculously easy.

When Mario Balotelli was at City, we'd have so much money by the end of the year – to be honest, we'd have so much money by the second week of February – that we could give the staff a much-deserved bonus and have a pretty spectacular Christmas do. There'd be £100,000 in there just from Mario being late. He didn't do it on purpose. He was just a bit dozy. Quite a lot of the time, he'd arrive on time for training, only to forget what time the meeting started or what room it was in. He'd be sitting somewhere else in the training ground, totally oblivious, and it would cost him a few thousand pounds.

No, it was a good system. It was a fair system. If I got fined, I wouldn't contest it. Most of the time, anyway. The problem was that I'm not a grass. I was one of the leaders of the dressing room, one of the most long-serving players, but I definitely wasn't going to snitch on someone for being late. The rules only really applied if Vincent caught you. And I wasn't going to go and do his dirty work for him, either. I'm not a teacher. I'm one of the guys. I wanted to be friends with everyone. I couldn't be going up to Mario Balotelli every other week and telling him I was docking his wages by £5,000 because he was in the canteen when he should have been in a video analysis session. So I'd find Mario, tell him we knew he was late, but let him off with a warning. A fierce look, a wagging finger, a plea not to do it again, and then telling him that I was going to let him off this time. It never worked, obviously. I'd have the same conversation with him a few days later. There was only so much I could do.

Occasionally, though, there would be a bit of a popular uprising. That was what took me and a few others to Vincent's immaculate locker, every now and again, with a pair of bolt-cutters. Like all dictators, he was obsessed with security. He was one of only two people who used to put a padlock on his locker; the other was Nedum Onuoha, who also had coursework stored in there. We'd make sure nobody was watching, snap the padlock off, and then empty the contents of Vincent's locker around the room. The work for his degree was unfortunate collateral damage. Nobody minded that Vincent was studying. But we had to get to that fine sheet and destroy it. Players know there have to be rules. That doesn't mean they always believe there should be consequences.

But those aren't the only guidelines that govern players' lives inside the game. There are a set of unwritten rules, too. Sometimes, they will make absolutely no sense, and might be rooted in nothing more than a manager's superstition. For reasons that I don't pretend to understand, Roberto Mancini hated the colour purple. He thought it was unlucky. I don't know where he'd got it from, but he was absolutely convinced of it, so he banned it from the training ground. It didn't affect me particularly, as a man who does not own that many violet clothes, but it meant that at least one of the club's tracksuits that year was effectively outlawed. I'm not sure what Umbro felt about that.

Others are to do with decency, more than anything. They don't come with a defined punishment – they're unofficial rules – other than risking the anger of the rest of the players. Some clubs will have set ideas, for example, on what sort of cars a player might be allowed to drive. At Manchester United, Sir Alex Ferguson never wanted to see the younger members of his squad pitching up at Carrington in supercars; he felt they needed to earn the right to be a little bit flash. Barcelona have a policy of only allowing players to arrive for training in club-issued cars; the sports cars and the SUVs have to stay at home.

We didn't have anything so concrete at City, but what we did have was a strict idea of what was suitable. Anyone turning up in a car that seemed to be a bit above their station would be told, in no uncertain terms, that they might want to tone it down a bit. Normally, the person who would deliver that message – in his usual calm, friendly manner – was Craig Bellamy. If a striker who was struggling for goals, or a young player who'd only made a couple of appearances for the first team, bowled up in an R8 or a Bentley, Craig would very gently take them aside and scream, 'What the fuck are you driving that for? You've only scored twice in the last three months!' right in their faces. That's the way these important traditions are passed down from generation to generation.

The rules don't stop when you leave the training ground, either. There is one more extremely important rule that every player immediately, instinctively understands. If 'Don't be late' is the first rule of football, the first rule of being a footballer is 'Don't get caught'.

When you go out, as a footballer, you learn pretty quickly that you have to move in silence. You can't go out as a big group: that's far too conspicuous. When you go to the clubs that have a reputation for being popular with players, you have to know how to get out without being spotted; in Manchester, you could assume that there would be paparazzi camped outside Panacea and M2 and Bedlam. You have to be smart. You have to be a little bit sly. You have to be subtle. As a young man on a Premier League wage, you can do pretty much anything you want. But you always have to remember that you must not get caught.

In the early days at City, that was pretty easy, thanks to Joey Barton. Joey is a difficult sort of person to describe. He is bright, funny, good company, and then a switch seems to flick and he is somebody completely different, somebody he cannot quite control. It's hard to have a lot of sympathy for him. A lot of his troubles have been nobody's fault but his own, and he's done some unforgivable things. But, from my own experience, I never had a problem with him. We got on well. He was good to me when I was first coming through.

All of those problems, though, meant that in the first couple of years of my career, he drew all of the attention. The papers wanted to know what Joey Barton was up to; they didn't really care about the rest of us. He was the biggest story at Manchester City. He was, before the take-over, basically the only story at Manchester City. That was absolutely fine by me.

We had a set routine for the week, depending on when we were playing. We would, 100 per cent, go out on a Saturday night, after a game. You might not always feel like it, if you'd lost that afternoon, but as long as you weren't playing on a Sunday, Saturday night was the big one. Then there were certain places we'd go on specific nights. It was Bedlam on a Tuesday, somewhere else if we were out on a Wednesday, another club if it was a Thursday. Often, it would be at least two of them. Sometimes, in a good week, all three.

It was a world I'd never seen before. A couple of years earlier I'd been a kid from Chapeltown in the academy, not earning much more than pocket money. My first professional deal was worth £500 a week. But once I was in the first team it was £5,000 a week. That's when your life starts changing, and that's when you start to think that you're going to start living. The fact that you're still under-age isn't a problem. Money solves a lot of problems at the doors to nightclubs, but it isn't as important as trust. As long as the security knew you wouldn't start any trouble, and as long as you could pay for a table, nobody seemed to ask for ID. And I wasn't going out to start trouble. I was going out to have a good time. I didn't want fights. I wanted a bottle of champagne with a sparkler sticking out of it.

Older players, the ones from previous generations, will often criticise younger ones for how much they go out, but I've always found that slightly strange. Players have always enjoyed a big night out or two (or three) during the week. The only difference now is that, rather than drinking a dozen pints, players tend to stick to champagne or vodka. They're still drinking, it's just that it isn't going to leave you feeling bloated and heavy the next day.

And when you're young, you can handle it. Most of the time, I didn't drink loads when I was out, but I was still staying up until three or four in the morning. The following day in training, though, I could still go and be the best player. You can handle a bit of a hangover when you're in your teens. You start to think that, actually, this being a footballer business is quite easy, really. You can go out as much as you like, drink as much as you need, and still be no worse for wear when you're doing your sprints.

We had to be a little bit more careful when the stakes changed at City, of course. After the takeover, as the money flooded in, bringing better players and higher ambitions and greater scrutiny with it, we no longer had the benefit of nobody being especially interested in what we were doing. There was, all of a sudden, a far greater chance of being caught. That didn't stop us, obviously. It just meant taking more precautions.

There was a summer when Manchester City took us on a pre-season tour to Los Angeles. Pre-season is incredibly important: it's when you build up your fitness to make sure that you're in good condition for the season ahead. But among players, there is a sense that it doesn't really count, not in terms of going out. There are no meaningful games. There's no *Super Sunday* around the corner, no titles on the line. So, thinking about it, taking the whole squad to Los Angeles is probably not the brightest move.

Roberto Mancini, the manager, had told us that we were allowed out for something to eat, as long as we made it back for curfew. We had to be back at the hotel for midnight. That was a bit of a shame, because that's when LA starts to come alive, and so we did what players always do: we came up with a plan to get around it. It was a good plan, too, one that involved me, David Silva, Nigel de Jong and Joleon Lescott shinning down the fire escape and clambering into a couple of taxis that were waiting for us below. We'd thought of every eventuality. We wore our club tracksuits in case we were caught. Now some people, people who aren't as good as were at sneaking out from under Roberto Mancini's nose, might say that was stupid, that it made it much more likely that we'd be spotted, but we knew better. If we got caught on the way out, we'd just say we were nipping out for a walk. Los Angeles is famous for what a wonderful city it is for a stroll. Nobody could object to us going out for a walk. We need not have worried, though. We made it out that night. I think David Silva was the last of us to get back at around 6 a.m. Nobody was better at not getting caught than

David Silva. He was quiet, dedicated, softly spoken, but he loved a beer.

He was part of our little group that summer. Players know full well that going out all together is a bad idea, so a squad tends to split up into smaller factions. It's easier to move in the shadows when there are only a few of you. In LA, you had one group made up of Joe Hart, Gareth Barry and James Milner, and a couple of others. Milner doesn't drink, famously, but that doesn't mean he doesn't like to have fun. They hired a boat at one point, and went out on that. Then you had the Eastern Europeans: a little clique of Aleksandar Kolarov, Edin Džeko, Stefan Savić. It sounds like a stereotype to say they'd go and find a dark bar to drink vodka in, but that is exactly what happened. And then you had our group: me, Nigel, Joleon, David, Gaël Clichy.

We had a couple of close calls. There was another night when Joleon, Nigel and I went out to a club. I'm not quite sure why, but we'd hired a car and chosen to drive. We knew LA quite well by that point, so had obviously decided it was the best idea. On the way back, we got pulled over by the police. As far as I could tell, our only offence was being three black guys in a nice car. That was enough for the LAPD. The sirens came on, they asked us to wind our windows down. We'd done nothing wrong, but we were lucky, I suppose, that we got away with nothing worse than a spurious speeding ticket.

Not everyone was included in those groups. You can play fast and loose with the rules if your position at a club is secure. You know that the punishment isn't going to be all that severe: you're too valuable to be cut out of the squad or sold or anything like that. There might be a fine, there might be a bit of a dressing-down, but that's it. If you're borderline, if you're worried that maybe the manager doesn't fancy you or that the club might be trying to buy a replacement, you have to be more careful. You don't need to give them an excuse.

Then there was Vincent, who had to take a bit of extra care, as captain, mainly because it would have been very awkward if he'd had to write his own name down on his little piece of paper and fine himself. I always felt a little sorry for him. I was just baffled by Sergio Agüero, who would do in Los Angeles what he did everywhere else: stay in, playing Xbox. And nobody wanted to go out with Balotelli, either. Not because he wasn't fun – a night out with Mario Balotelli would obviously be a lot of fun – but because he was a risk factor. It wasn't just that he was a law unto himself, unpredictable, almost dangerous, but because he was too high-profile. Everyone wanted to know what Balotelli, the bad boy of European football, would do next. Set off fireworks at home? Set off fireworks in my home? Hand out money at a petrol station? Walk a live tiger through the streets of a major city? People were watching his every move, and if you hang around with him, that means they'll be watching your every move, too. That money, that fame, that reputation: it was too much. Players will stay away from that, because they know the first rule of being a footballer almost as well as they know the first rule of football. Whatever happens, don't get caught.

4

57 MILES TO OLDHAM

No matter how hard they try to be subtle, scouts are not hard to spot. The person standing on the touchline that nobody in the team knows? The one who isn't someone's dad or uncle or friend from down the road, but is spending their Saturday morning watching a load of 12-year-olds play football? The one wearing a huge padded coat, regardless of the weather, the sort that Arsène Wenger used to have such trouble zipping up? That'll be a scout.

Some of them don't even make an effort to be discreet. Leeds City Boys was a sort of holding pen for all the kids in Leeds who hadn't been picked up early by Leeds United. If you weren't quite good enough to get through a trial at Leeds, if you were one of the best players for your school or for a local club team, then you'd get invited to play for Leeds City Boys. We were a bit like the Harlem Globetrotters, except that we were all 11, and we spent our Saturday afternoons hanging out in the McDonald's at the bottom of Briggate, stealing straws. We had some incredible players. It's not especially surprising, given that we had a team of the best players in the city, that we battered almost everyone we played against.

Dr Towers, the teacher who ran the team, was unbelievable at getting scouts to come and watch. He saw it as his job to give us all the best possible chance of making it, and he'd earned a reputation as a talent-spotter. If he said he had a player worth checking out, then people were inclined to believe him: David Batty, Brian Deane and Alan Smith – not the Sky one, the other one – had all started out at Leeds City Boys. It was an incredible honour even to be part of the team. I'd only been given a chance because my primary school teacher, Mr Moore, had taken it upon himself to put my name forward. He'd seen how good I was on the playground, and he believed in me enough to think I could make it. I have never forgotten how much I owe Mr Moore.

There were scouts at pretty much every game we played. Not from Leeds, necessarily, and often not from major Premier League teams, but from the clubs that had to be a bit more creative, the ones that maybe had to cast their nets just a little wider: Blackburn and Oldham, Preston and Bradford. A lot of the time, they didn't try to hide it. They'd come along with a huge badge sewn onto their enormous coat. Even an 11-year-old can work out what that guy with the massive Blackburn badge on his chest might be doing.

There'd be a bit of a buzz among the players whenever we knew, for certain, that a scout was watching, but other than that I was basically oblivious to it. After games, they wouldn't come and talk to the player: they'd go and search out one or both of their parents, to try to do a bit of due diligence on what the kid was like. They'd ask where they were from, where they lived, what the family set-up was. If they were really interested, they'd try and work out how dedicated the kid might be, whether they had offers from other clubs, what they were thinking about the future.

That happened to me, too, but I didn't know anything about it at the time. My dad used to come and watch every single one of my games, and he never breathed a word about any of it to me. He didn't tell me that this club was watching me, or that there was a chance to go here. He didn't encourage me to show off a bit more, so I could earn myself a move, even if it wasn't in the best interests of the team.

He wasn't the sort of parent to push me. He didn't shout from the touchline about what I was doing wrong. He didn't try and give me advice. He's adamant to this day that he was a much better player than me, he'd just never been given the chance to prove it after he moved over to Leeds from St Kitts (he'd hurt his knee as a kid doing gymnastics, landing badly from a pommel horse, and he never recovered). He's not joking. He's deadly serious. But even then, he never tried to live through me. Football wasn't his way of passing on his dream.

To an extent, he never had to say anything. I don't remember my dad ever shouting at me. Not because I was an angel – I wasn't – but because as soon as he was around, I was instinctively well behaved. He had a presence. An aura. I never wanted to disappoint him. It's the reason I never got a tattoo, or earrings. He never said anything about it. He never told me I wasn't allowed them. I was just worried he wouldn't approve, and that was enough. It was the same with football. He didn't have to criticise things I'd done wrong for me to want to improve them. I wanted to impress him. I wanted to get better for him. Just him being there was an inspiration to me, though I don't know if I ever told him, and I don't know if he ever knew. All he wanted was for me to enjoy playing football. That was the best thing he could have done for me: he just let me play.

Not every parent is like that. There are an awful lot of talented young players who have their careers ruined by that one family member – could be a dad, could be a mum, could be a brother or an uncle or whoever – who knows everything. They know everything about what a player should be doing, and what a coach should be doing, too. They're just a little bit too loud on the touchline. They know everything about what contracts they should sign, about what team they should play for, about what move they should make. They tend to start wearing a massive padded coat, too, but deep down they're using their own child's hobby to play out a fantasy of being Jorge Mendes. In most cases, they make so many ridiculous demands and give their children such bad advice that they spoil their chances of making it.

I was lucky. My dad didn't do any of that. I wouldn't have been a player without him, I'm certain of that. Or, at least, I wouldn't have been the player I was. If he'd tried to interfere, there's a good chance that my career would have gone in a very different direction, or no direction at all. He did everything he could to help me. He made huge sacrifices to allow me to go as far as I could. He put himself under incredible pressure, but he did it so that I didn't feel any.

Once you've made it, once you've become a professional, you find that there are a surprising number of people who have decided they helped you on the way. All sorts of people, friends of the family and friends of friends and sometimes complete strangers, will pull you aside and ask if you remember when they took you to training, when they came to your games, when they played a small but vital role in enabling you to become successful. The problem is that I know full well who helped me make it. Sometimes my uncle Eric took me to training, or my old teacher Mr Moore. Sometimes some friends of ours in Manchester looked after me. But most of the time, it was my dad, and nobody else.

It was my dad who drove me to Oldham, the club that we'd decided was the next best step after Leeds City Boys. It was an hour or so on the motorway from Wetherby, a middle-class market town outside Leeds where I went to school. He'd pick me up in his banged-out Vauxhall Astra or his battered Renault Megane or, sometimes, just the van he had for work. It would be me, him and my little brother Meshech, two or three times a week, playing whatever daft games he could invent. He'd make us guess what the distance would be when we came to the next road sign. That was fun, the first time we played it. The second and the third and the fortieth, you already know the answer. I can still recite all of the mileages on that stretch of the M62, even now.

When we told him that was boring, he'd put some music on, some reggae or some dancehall or some bashment or some spiritual music, and every so often he'd turn it down and tell us to listen to the lyrics, to understand what the song was trying to say. We'd point out that at the age of 11 or 12 all we really cared about was the beat. Even that was better than the alternative, though, which was being trapped in a car on a clogged-up motorway as my dad tried to give us an impromptu talk on sex education. I don't know who's meant to do that, whether it's better coming from a mum or from a dad, but it's definitely not meant to come from *my* dad. It would come out of nowhere: you're quietly trying to remember if it's 42 or 36 miles to Oldham and all of a sudden you can hear your dad using the words 'pubic hair'. We'd squirm into our seats, desperate to escape. If there's anything in the world you don't want to hear, it's your dad talking about pubes while you're in an enclosed space.

He wouldn't always come and watch me once we'd got there. There were times when he'd stay in the car and fall asleep, the only time he ever gave me a glimpse of what he was putting himself through so that I had a chance to make it.

As a teenager, you don't always have your priorities right. Rolling up at Oldham in my dad's van didn't exactly mark me out as one of the cool kids. Even then, some of the players who came from better-off backgrounds or nicer areas would be dropped off for training in their parents' Range Rovers. There were a couple who always had the latest Predators, too. You can tell a lot about a player by the boots they wear. There was a strict hierarchy. You wore the boots that suited the sort of player you were, and the best players wore the best boots.

Predators tended to mean you were technical. You probably took the free-kicks. You had to wear the Predators so you could get the whip and the curve on the ball. If you wore white boots, that meant you were quick: a winger, a flying full-back, a darting striker. You couldn't wear white boots and be a lumbering central defender, or a plodding central midfielder. If you went colourful – blue and yellow and silver and green – then you were creative. A number 10. You saw things other players didn't, including a reason to wear green boots. Nobody wore black boots, because wearing black boots was basically admitting that you weren't quick, or technical, or creative. Wearing black boots was a sign to all of the other players that you were going to end up as a right-back, and nobody dreams of being a right-back.

That hierarchy held all the way from Leeds City Boys up to being a professional: I remember the first time I ever played against Philippe Coutinho, in a pre-season friendly when he was still at Inter Milan, I noticed there was a little guy wearing ridiculously bright boots. I knew straightaway that he'd be good. You couldn't wear boots that bold and not have a few tricks up your sleeve.

My boots were always a bit of an exception. We couldn't afford to have the best, brightest, newest boots. Instead, I got all of mine from a shop called Donnay Sports in Leeds. Most of the time, I was wearing some Jimmy Grimbles, whatever Umbros I could get my hands on: big, bulky, ugly things, the cheapest actual boots you could buy, in whatever colour they had in stock. Even when I upgraded a bit, it was for a knock-off version. For a while, the boot everyone wanted was the R9, named after Ronaldo, the Brazilian striker and the best player on the planet until Lionel Messi and Cristiano Ronaldo came along.

They were a thing of beauty, the R9s: blue and silver, light and sleek. They were, though, not available in Donnay Sports. Instead, they had a cheaper take on the R9. The colours weren't quite as vibrant. The leather wasn't quite as soft. The Nike tick looked like it had been drawn on by a child, and not even an especially gifted child. You could tell they were knock-off Nigels from the moment you saw them. Everyone at Oldham would have known they were snide, but nobody dared say anything. I was quicker than everyone else, technically better than everyone else, and more creative than everyone else, even with a pair of knock-off boots on my feet. I was the best player there. Those boots were the only thing levelling the playing field. Imagine how good I could have been with some proper Predators.

Like my dad's car, my boots could have been a source of embarrassment for me. Kids are competitive. They worry about status. But none of it ever bothered me. I knew how hard he was working to get me to training, and that was much more important to me than the car we drove in or the boots I wore. He was a grafter, my dad. He'd get up at half four for work – he did the electrics for Adshel, a name you'll recognise from bus stops – and after a full day, he'd come and pick me up and take me to Oldham. He had to borrow money from uncles and friends to pay for the petrol, just to get me to training, but he never once complained, never once said that it was too much. A lot of the kids I knew didn't know their dads. The fact that he was only ever absent occasionally – normally when he was in Ethiopia, doing charity work – meant a lot to me. The fact he was around at all was enough.

It was important, too. Oldham proved to be the perfect choice for me. There had been a lot of clubs sniffing around, but my dad felt it was the best fit. It was half an hour closer to home than Manchester, and it had a real family feel to it. It wasn't an academy, but a school of excellence: it was a step up from Leeds City Boys, but not a step too far. There was a clear pathway to the first team. We had a Dutch coach, who was tactically and technically different to anything I'd worked with before. That was just what I needed. You don't think you're definitely going to make it when you sign for a club like Oldham, but you feel like you maybe have a chance.

That doesn't go unnoticed. It isn't just club scouts who are looking for players almost as soon as they hit their teens. Agents are, too. The most obviously talented players, the ones who are clearly destined to make it, might have an agent acting on their behalf by the time they're 14. (Their parents might also suddenly have jobs with a major Premier League team, employed as an extremely well-paid gardener or something.) But they descend on anyone who shows even a little bit of promise before that, and they will use anything they can to reel you in.

I heard countless pitches from agents when I was at Oldham, and then even more once I'd signed for Manchester City. They'll tell you anything they think you want to hear. They'll present you with a map of what your career would look like under their influence. You sign representation deals for a couple of years, but they look much further into the future. They'll explain how you'll get to your first pro contract at 17, and what you should be expecting to earn at that point. Then it will be from 17 until 19 or 20, when you'll be breaking into the first team, and again, how much you should be paid at that stage in your career. Then it will be your first major deal, becoming a first-team regular, earning your first transfer, England recognition, all of it: a picture of the ideal career, from start to finish, and a promise of the millions you'll earn in the process if only you sign with them.

Then they'll talk to you about all of the money you can make off the pitch. They'll tell you that not only can they get you a sponsorship deal, but that they alone can get you a better sponsorship deal than anyone else. They'll tell you that they have special connections at one of the main brands, the glamorous ones, Nike or Adidas or Puma or Donnay Sports, and that there's a deal waiting for you just as soon as you sign.

That's just the start. They pepper you with questions about what you're interested in. It could be fashion or gaming or modelling or aftershave or jewellery, and then they'll go into detail about what other sorts of endorsements are out there, and tell you about all of the other opportunities that they can offer you over the course of your career. They'll explain to you how much money you can make from all of the extra-curricular activities if you play for a mid-table team, and how much more it would be if you played for a team that's competing for titles or the Champions League. They'll tell you that playing for Manchester United is where the big money is. You're worth a lot more to a brand if you're a Manchester United player than almost anyone else.

That's just the pitch, the official offer to persuade you to join up. There are plenty of other ways agents try to convince players to hand them their business, their career, their life. I was offered huge sums of money to sign with certain agencies. Some said they would buy my parents a house if I joined them.

Others wine and dine you. One agent made a point of picking me up from my home in Chapeltown in his sports car and taking me for a meal at Bibi's, a fancy Italian restaurant in the middle of Leeds. It was the sort of place where we could never have afforded to eat, but there I was, at 14 or 15, being told to have three courses if I wanted. It makes you feel special. It makes you feel as if you've made it, or as though you definitely will make it if you let this obvious high-roller take charge of your career. It is not just meals. The same agent took me to a strip club in Leeds, too. I wasn't 18 at the time. I don't think I was 16. It's meant to impress you, to offer you a little taste of the lifestyle they're promising you: supercars and strippers and a world where the rules don't really apply.

That's not the only way they show their clout. I ended up signing, when I was 16, for a well-known agent called

Jerome Anderson. He represented some of the biggest and best players in the country. He was a major player, back then, respected and respectable. He had a good reputation. He had credibility. He wanted me to know that.

Most agents have at least one high-profile client, someone who is a top man at their club, and they often use them to act as a kind of advert for their services. Jerome Anderson knew I was an Arsenal fan as a kid, so as he was trying to convince me to join him he got Ian Wright to give me a call. Wrighty didn't try and sell me anything. He just said that he'd heard I was doing really well, encouraged me to work hard, and then said that he'd always been really pleased with what Jerome had done for him. He didn't guarantee me that signing with Jerome would get me a move to Arsenal or make me an England international, just that in his experience he'd always been brilliant. I don't know if I said anything in return; it's quite a strange experience, being a 16-year-old and suddenly finding yourself on the phone to one of your childhood heroes. You can't ask intelligent questions or pin him down on what his agent's commercial strategy has been. You're just buzzing that Ian Wright has got your phone number.

The charm offensive didn't stop there. Through Ian, they sorted me out with a signed Thierry Henry shirt. Henry had always been my favourite player. I still have it. It's one of my most prized possessions, but it was a way for Jerome to show me what sort of clout he had, what sort of influence, what a powerful figure I'd have in my corner if he represented me. It worked. I signed for him.

I felt I could handle all of that because I had my dad, a strong character behind me, helping me, advising me. My dad wasn't taken in by the promises and he wasn't fooled by the bluster. He wasn't especially loud or confrontational and he never thought he knew more than anyone else. Quietly and gently, though, he steered me away from the people he didn't trust and towards the ones he felt were more reliable, the ones who might even at times have my best interests at heart, rather than their own.

In a lot of cases, that's the last thing an agent wants. There are times when parents and family members get in the way of a player's career. That's definitely true. Sometimes, it will at least be for the right reasons: they will be trying to protect their son or daughter, and just going about it the wrong way. In those cases, I can see why agents might see families as a problem, and why they might feel they have to tell young players to listen to the person who has experience in the industry, understands the game, and knows how things work.

But there were also plenty of times when agents did all they could to keep my dad out of things. They'd ask to meet me, separately, away from him, because they knew I listened to him and that if he didn't like them, then there wasn't a chance I'd join them. They'd tell me that of course he had my best interests at heart. He's my dad. It's just that he doesn't know football. He doesn't know how to get things done. He might be your dad, and he might be good at it, but you need an agent, and he's not an agent.

That puts you in an impossible position. You're being asked to choose between your family and what you think is your career. It feels, at times, like the two things are completely separate. The agent might have a roster of impressive clients. They might be able to point to a dozen players whose careers they've shaped. They have a track record. They can promise to do exactly the same for you. But the price is that you have to stop listening to your mum or your dad or whoever it might be, who might want what is best for you, but has never shaped a career or established a reputation or built a track record. For a teenager, that's an incredibly difficult situation to be caught in. What winds me up the most about it is that, in a lot of cases, agents will deliberately place a youngster in that position, simply because they need the parents and the relatives out of the way, so that they can make money from you.

It didn't work with me. I always listened to my dad. We didn't always make the right choices, and there were definitely times, looking back, when I might have done things differently, but I wonder what would have happened if my dad hadn't been there, if he hadn't had such a clear idea of what the right thing to do was. I would have been ripped off left, right and centre.

Agents prey on the vulnerable. Most kids, dreaming of being footballers, wanting to make it more than anything else, are vulnerable. And most families, knowing that their child might be able to make more money than they have ever seen, hearing about all of the sponsorships and endorsement deals and contract offers that will definitely be coming their way – just as soon as they've signed down here, just there, initial there – to make them financially secure for generations, are vulnerable, too. For any family, having all of that dangled in front of them, it must be incredibly difficult not to get sucked in.

That would be fine, if so many of those promises didn't prove to be empty. There's one thing that no agent ever thinks to mention, not really, and that is that everything they're promising depends on what you do on the pitch. The career that they painstakingly lay out for you is irrelevant if you don't do the business in games. They can't guarantee you a first-team contract at 18 or a big move when you're 22.

The brands aren't interested in you until you're a household name. Agents don't have boot deals lined up for most 14-year-olds. They might be able to get you a few bits of equipment as a gesture of goodwill, to butter you up for a deal down the road, but the big money will only appear when you're a first-team regular, someone the brands see a bit of value in. As the current face and voice of webuyanycar.com, I can tell you that the other endorsements only come along later, when you're established, and even then they may not materialise. I'd always had my eye on doing a bit of modelling: when I was 18 and flying, playing not just for Manchester City but England, too, I thought that I might stand a bit of a chance of cracking the *Men's Health* market. Fine, nobody's going to want to take close-up pictures of my face, but I was in good shape. Calvin Klein was the dream. Djimon Hounsou, the actor who'd become famous in the Leonardo DiCaprio film *Blood Diamond*, had done a campaign for them, and I reckon I stacked up nicely next to him. It was the sort of thing an agent would promise they could help sort out. I'm still waiting. Feel free to get in touch.

It felt to me, a lot of the time, like I was doing my job and they weren't really doing theirs. That is the thing with a lot of agents: as soon as they have your signature, as soon as they have your business, their interest wanes. Until there's another contract to renegotiate, that is, or until there's a transfer to be handled. Everything in between, though, depends on how you perform. The agent is not in control of it, no matter what they tell you and your family to get you to sign. You have to do all of the work. You have to make it all happen. There is no blueprint. There is no map. It's all uncharted territory, and you have to pick your own way through it. I heard so many agents tell me how it was all going to play out, as though everything would be set when I signed that first professional deal. I learned pretty quickly that it doesn't work like that at all.

5

PERI-PERI SPICE MIX

Stephen Ireland would have got away with it, if only he'd remembered that the one thing that Micah Richards knows more than anything – more than football, more than where to go out on a weeknight in Manchester, more than the mileage signs between Wetherby and Oldham – is chicken.

When we first broke through into the first team at Manchester City, a group of us lived on the same development in Warrington. They were all nice houses, but Stephen had the nicest of the lot. He had the grand one, the centrepiece of the development. Maybe that was because he was that little bit older and had been playing for a little bit longer, so he'd saved up a bit more cash, or maybe it was because Stephen wasn't particularly shy about spending it. He was the man with the pink Baby Bentley, after all.

One week, he decided that he wanted to have a few of us over for dinner. That's not the sort of invitation you generally get from a fellow player. They might invite you on a night out. They might decide that they want to sort a table at a club. They very rarely suggest you all get together for a chat over candles and wine, particularly when you're all in your late teens and they're Stephen Ireland. But he was adamant: he wanted a group of us to come to his place to eat. Stranger still, he declared that he was going to cook.

That raised a few eyebrows. We didn't want to judge, but Stephen Ireland didn't really strike anyone as much of a genius in the kitchen. It seemed unlikely that he'd been a gifted chef, and just hadn't thought to mention it. There was, I would say, a pretty high risk that we'd all go to his house for dinner and come back with food poisoning. Still, we went. We were too intrigued to turn the offer down.

When we got there, he'd pulled out all of the stops. The food was carefully presented on his finest china. It was all neatly arranged: marinated chicken, twice-cooked chips, some vegetables. But like I say: I know chicken. I'd go as far as to say that I'm a chicken connoisseur. And I knew, from the first bite, that this wasn't some ancient family recipe, passed down to Stephen from one of his many grandmothers, including a secret blend of herbs and spices. I know a Nando's when I taste one, and there was no doubt in my mind that this was Nando's. It wasn't even a peri-peri spice mix that you buy in the supermarket, to recreate that recognisable taste from the comfort of your own kitchen. This was takeaway Nando's. He'd got the food delivered, taken it out of the boxes, served it out on plates, and was now pretending to all of us that he'd cooked it. Maybe it would have worked, if he'd invited a different group of players. Maybe it would have been fine, if he'd made the offer to some people who didn't know their way around chicken. Instead, he'd been rumbled. Not that we said anything, of course. He'd gone to such an effort. He seemed so proud of himself. We didn't want to embarrass him. We told him the chicken was great. Nobody asked for the recipe.

Those were the glory days, possibly the best days of my career. Not in terms of trophies and titles and fame and recognition: all of that came later. But those first couple of seasons, after establishing myself in the first team but before the money poured into Manchester City, were probably the happiest I had in football.

I'd moved to City in 2001 after a couple of years at Oldham. In a way, I would have liked more time at Oldham: it was a comfortable environment, a friendly one, and I was settled there. I knew, though, that I had to make the leap if I was to see how far I could get in football. I'd been the best player at Oldham by a distance: that, presumably, was what had attracted City's attention.

As soon as I arrived, I was right back at the start. Compared with the players I was up against, I was almost totally raw. That wasn't really all that surprising. At Oldham, we'd trained a couple of times a week, and then had a game at the weekend. At City, they trained every day. The facilities were better, and so were the players. They were fitter than me. They were faster than me. Everything was one touch, two touch. I could have lost heart, worried that I'd been found out. That was a delicate moment. I was 14. I'd moved away from home. I was living in a new city, surrounded by people I didn't know, and it would have been easy to look at the standard of player around me and give up. I could have lost heart, worried that I'd been found out.

That was never how I thought. I would guess that's not how any player who ends up as a professional thinks. Instead, I looked at all of those players who were miles ahead of me and decided that they wouldn't be able to say that for long. I was fortunate that the club had sent me to live in digs in Gatley, with a couple called Paul and Kath Priest. Paul was a devoted City fan, and his family regularly hosted academy kids. They kept me from feeling any homesickness. They didn't even mind when they found the little stash of adult films I kept hidden under the DVD player in my room. I was cringing, but they laughed it off. Most importantly, I had a room to have a DVD player in: I'd been sleeping on the floor of my little brother's room for a few months at home, after my older brother split up with his partner and moved back in. It would be totally natural to feel overwhelmed as a teenager, moving so far from home, but to me it felt like luxury.

It was a good time to be at Manchester City as a young player. There's a reason that teams regularly competing for titles and playing in the Champions League struggle to produce their own players. Their squads are full of the best players in the world in their positions, so they might be able to find a spot for a ready-made superstar – someone like Phil Foden or Trent Alexander-Arnold, a player who has enough talent to slot straight in as a teenager – but they won't be able to give game time to a youngster who needs a little work, a little space to iron out the flaws in their game. The level is too high. Besides, young players make mistakes, and the last thing a manager trying to win the Premier League, a manager expected to end the season with at least one trophy, needs is mistakes.

Instead, the best place for a young player can often be at a club just below that level: Everton had a long run of producing quality players from their academy, and Manchester City was the same when I arrived. The staff were fantastic. I knew one of the coaches already: Pete Lowe had left Oldham to join City, and I always suspected that he was the one who had encouraged the club to take a look at me. But he was not the only one who did everything they could to help you make it: Frankie Bunn, Alex Gibson and Paul Power, all of them working under Jim Cassell, were as expert and as dedicated as you could want. It wasn't just that they wanted you to fulfil your potential. It wasn't just that they wanted to be able to say that they were producing players for the club. It was that Manchester City, at the time, needed to be able to bring players through. It was in a position at the time where it could afford to take chances on young players. Or, maybe, it couldn't afford not to take chances. There wasn't the money available to stock the squad full of the best players on the planet. That created a pathway, one that was illustrated on the walls of the academy. There were pictures of all of the players who had come through everywhere you looked, an advert and an inspiration to all of the kids hoping to make the same journey. These pictures made you feel like that dream of yours really was possible. The most recent image belonged to Shaun Wright-Phillips, who had made it into the first team and won the club's young player of the year award four years in a row. I was part of the group aiming to follow in his footsteps.

There were quite a few of us. Nedum Onuoha, the man everyone called 'Chief', was the golden boy. Not just because of the player he was – a composed, calm, rapid defender – but because of how bright he was. Nedum was a genius. He was the sort of boy anyone would be proud to take home to meet their parents: intelligent, well-educated, polite. Everyone at the academy loved him, and everyone was pretty sure he would make it all the way.

Stephen Ireland was the same age as him but, and let's put this nicely, a very different sort of a person. He'd not spent years at City's academy. They'd signed him from a team in Ireland when he was 15. Then there was Michael Johnson, a year younger but, if anything, even more talented. He was a playmaker, full of ideas, and he looked destined for the top. Ishmael Miller, a striker, was part of my little group. There was him, me, and Kelvin Etuhu, a dynamic midfielder, though I was younger than both of them. Finally, the youngest of the lot was Daniel Sturridge, another forward. He was quiet, Daniel. He lived with his family outside Manchester. When we started going out, Daniel didn't come. He was that little bit younger, which may have made a difference, but I think he had a more serious, more dedicated attitude, too. He had that professional mindset from a young age. He was determined to be the best he could be. Everything else took a back seat.

We were all pretty much the same age. We had all been on much the same journey. We had all been through the same things, dealt with the same challenges, overcome the same problems. We all got along. We should, really, have been allies. We should have had each other's backs. That's how you imagine it is, when you see something like the Class of '92 come through. It looks, from the outside, like a group of friends all sharing the same dream.

Football does not work like that. It is brutal and it is cut-throat. You are a team but you're not a team. The most important thing to any player is their own ambition, their own desire to make it, and that can make it very difficult to have friends in the way that most people understand it. You have mates, of course. You build relationships, ones that last for years. You develop a bond with the people you came through with. But it's not straightforward. You have to grow up pretty quickly. There's no room for emotion or loyalty. These people are your friends, but they're also your rivals.

It's impossible, for example, to be truly close to someone who shares your position. I tended to hang around with Ishmael and Kelvin partly because we shared the same agent, but mainly because neither of them were directly competing with me for a chance. But to Ish, someone like Sturridge was a threat. If Michael Johnson succeeded, maybe that would mean Kelvin wouldn't. For me, it was Nedum. I liked Nedum. My parents would have loved Nedum. But I knew that Nedum was standing in my way of getting into the first team. He was meant to be the next off the production line, the club's first-choice defender-in-waiting. Deep down, I didn't really want Nedum to succeed. Nedum establishing himself meant that I might never have a chance to do the same. And likewise, Nedum knew that if I kept improving, he might find himself knocked down a level. I might leapfrog him. I might take the chance that he'd spent years working towards. It didn't affect how I saw him as a person, but it's impossible to pretend that it didn't change our relationship. Nedum and I were in direct competition. My success wasn't in his interests, and his success wasn't in mine.

The way our careers played out illustrates that perfectly. Nedum did break into the first team earlier than me. He and Danny Mills were, for a while, Manchester City's two right-backs. But then they both got injured at the same time, and I got called up. My chance came at his expense. I took it, and from that point on he was no longer ahead of me in the pecking order. Football doesn't do sentiment.

The fact there was a group of us definitely helped with that transition from the academy to the first team, though. That doesn't happen overnight. Often, the best young players at a club will be invited up to train with the seniors a couple of times a week. You move backwards and forwards between the two, in the hope that not only do you get better from being exposed to senior players, but that it helps you settle in when you eventually make the leap full-time.

That first sight of the first team is intimidating. It's easy to joke about how bad Manchester City were in the days before the takeover, to pick out some of the banter signings they made, to act as though the whole squad was full of people like Danny Tiatto and David Sommeil, but even those teams had some great players. True, they might not quite have been at their absolute peak by the time they got to City, but to a teenager who'd been watching them on TV just a couple of years before, seeing them in the flesh was unnerving. As a kid, I was never overwhelmed by anything. I was completely fearless. I always assumed that I belonged. It never occurred to me that something might be a step too far, or that I'd not be good enough to keep up. But even I found myself a little quieter than normal when I realised I was training with Robbie Fowler, Steve McManaman and Nicolas Anelka. Even some of the less famous names – Sylvain Distin, Richard Dunne, Trevor Sinclair – were players who had been in the Premier League for years. It's the moment you've spent years waiting for, but when it comes it's quite hard to believe it's real.

I was too nervous to introduce myself to anyone. I filed silently into the changing room, got ready, and then walked out to the pitch without saying a word. I wasn't worried that I wouldn't be good enough, but I was worried about doing or saying the wrong thing. I was in my own head. I didn't want anyone to assume I was arrogant. I didn't want them to take against me. I didn't want to upset the wrong person, and in this case the wrong person was almost definitely Joey Barton. I wanted to fit in, and I wanted them to get to know the real me, but most of all I didn't want to blow my chance of being called up again. I was scared to do anything that might make the coaches think that I wasn't the right sort of character to have around. Those first few training sessions are a test:

not just of how good you are, but how you fit into that environment. I didn't want to fail.

Kevin Keegan, the manager at the time, obviously noticed. I was doing the warm-up runs with a hat on. All of a sudden, he pointed at me and shouted: 'You! You! Why have you got a hat on?' He made it sound like there was some rule I'd broken. I didn't know. Maybe in the first team wearing a hat was forbidden. Maybe it was the wrong sort of hat. Maybe it would have been OK if I'd been wearing a Stetson, or one of those Australian ones with the corks on it. I started to panic. I was looking around, sweating, stuttering an apology, when he started laughing. The rest of the squad were laughing, too. He was joking. He wanted to try and break the ice.

Being there, though, was not the same as belonging. It would be wrong to say that every single one of the senior players was hostile to the academy kids when they first appeared. Every player is different. More importantly, they all have slightly different places in the dressing-room hierarchy. They're all part of separate tribes. Richard Dunne was very much a captain. He saw it as his job to help people settle in. But then he could afford to be welcoming, because he knew his place in the team – and in the hierarchy – was secure. Sylvain Distin was a little tougher to crack. We didn't see eye to eye straightaway. I always felt he talked down to me, just a bit. He'd tell me that I could learn from the way he looked after himself, the way he trained, the way he ate. At 18, I maybe wasn't all that receptive to this sort of advice. It felt to me as if he was treating me like a child. And possibly just a little like he was in love with himself. It took me a while to realise that he was trying to help, just like Dunne was, only in his own special way. Distin wanted to make sure I didn't waste my talent. It was a form of tough love. And maybe it had to be just a little tough, because he'd have known that, ultimately, I was there to take his place.

Nobody was as good with me, though, as Trevor Sinclair. He was a City fan, Trevor, and though he'd go on to play for quite a long time after he left the club, he was coming to the end of his career. He took it upon himself to take me under his wing, to look after me, to make sure I was as prepared as I could be for what was about to happen. He took me to meet his agent, Neil Fewings, because he wanted to make sure I had the best person in my corner. There was no pressure: he was just trying to guide me. He told me that if there was anything I needed, anything at all, I just had to ask him. He'd sort everything out. Most importantly, he was brilliant with my dad. They became really close. My dad would pick Trevor's brains about the way I was being treated, about contracts, about what should be happening in my career and what was actually happening in my career. Trevor arranged for 50 shirts and loads of balls to be sent out to Ethiopia, where my dad did a lot of charity work. Nobody asked him to. I'm not even sure how he found out about it. He just did it out of the goodness of his heart.

Unfortunately, they stand out because they were the exceptions. You couldn't describe the welcome a young player gets from the vast majority of a senior squad as warm. Or you couldn't back then, anyway. I don't mean that the older pros were a bit frosty. They weren't sceptic-al. They didn't keep their cards close to their chests, wait-ing for you to prove yourself, and then give you a manly handshake to show that you'd been accepted. They were not trying to nurture you, to help you along. They were trying to break you. Fans love it when their team has a homegrown star. They love thinking that there's one of their own out on the pitch. They love knowing that they haven't had to pay a penny to bring them in. It's a feelgood story for everyone. Everyone, that is, except for the first team, the established players, the senior squad. They don't like a young player. They want you to fail. And most of them do everything they can to make that happen.

They are, as a rule, horrible to young players. They were horrible on a general level. They would do everything they could to belittle you, to make sure you knew that you were at the bottom of the pecking order. You'd be told not to go into a meeting or a training session or the canteen, because you had to wait until the older players had gone through before it was your turn. They went first. You went last. That was where you belonged. If you had a difficult train-ing session, or you weren't quite settling in, they didn't give you the benefit of the doubt. They didn't encourage you. They didn't try to bring you out of your shell. They just told you they thought you were shit. They made sure you felt like an outcast.

And they were horrible on a personal level, too. I started training with the first team when I was 16, and from almost the first day, Willo Flood decided that he wouldn't be calling me Micah. Instead, he'd call me 'Muca'. I had to google it to find out what it meant. It turns out it's a Gaelic word. It means 'shit'.

He called me that, without fail, for months, maybe longer. He was a first teamer, a relatively senior player, so I felt I couldn't really say anything. I didn't want to be seen as too sensitive. I didn't want people to think I couldn't take a bit of banter. That's the worst thing you can do. It's seen as a weakness, and any weakness at all is exploited. One day, though, Willo went too far. He said something else to me. I can't remember what it was – it may not even have been that bad, I'd just got to the end of my patience – but I snapped. I'm a happy person. I don't mind people having a laugh at my expense. But I'm also a kid from Chapeltown, and kids from Chapeltown don't take a lot of shit. There's a point at which a switch goes in my head, and Willo had reached it. I told him that if he ever spoke to me like that again, I'd get him in the dressing room and I'd beat him to a pulp. It was a bit of a risk. Willo was quite tough. He could look after himself. But he obviously realised I was serious. He stopped calling me Muca after that.

The strangest thing about the whole thing was that Willo wasn't a horrible person. He was, it turned out, really nice. He wasn't behaving like that because it was how he would naturally behave; he was behaving like that because it was how he felt he had to behave. It was the same for a lot of the older players, the ones who made life unpleasant for any young kid that appeared in the squad. They treated you like that because it was how they thought senior players had to treat younger ones; they treated you like that because it was how they'd been treated when they first came through. They'd come in as nervous teenagers and been bullied and intimidated by the previous generation, who themselves had probably found football incredibly hostile when they first came through. The abuse was passed downwards.

I hope that's changed now. It always seemed to me like the older players who I first encountered as a teenager had a lot of anger inside them. Clubs didn't really think about their players' mental health, as they're starting to do today. There weren't psychologists that you could visit if you felt it might help. You weren't encouraged to talk about your fears or your nerves or the pressure you were under. Nobody wanted to show anything that could be seen as weakness. Being a footballer is a privileged life in a lot of ways, but a dressing room is an unforgiving environment. It would be the last place on Earth you'd want to be if you were struggling with something. Now, I think players do have more help available, although that may not be enough to convince some of them to use it. I think clubs try to create a healthier culture. I think older players are more understanding with younger ones. That's in the best interests of the game as a whole. Quite a lot of those players who didn't make it, the ones who fell by the wayside and who were seen as cautionary tales, might have stood a better chance if they'd had some support, if they hadn't found the game quite as unwelcoming.

The thing that changed everything for me was making my debut. I'd been playing for England's Under-16s and Under-18s for years, but that didn't matter in the slightest to the older players at City. All that counted was being able to say that you were a Premier League player. Once that happened, your status changed. Almost overnight. The following week, you can almost feel that the senior players have accepted you. There's that little bit more respect. All of a sudden, you're not at the back of the queue anymore. You're one of them. Football is cut-throat, but it's also fickle. Once the players have worked out that you can help them, that you make them better, then you're in. Once you've made your debut, life gets a lot easier.

If, like me, you get to have two debuts, then so much the better. My first came in an away game at Arsenal. It was a bit of a free hit, really. Stuart Pearce had taken over from Keegan by that stage, and he was much more interested in the talent coming out of the academy. He would come to every reserve game to keep an eye on how we were developing. It felt like he was on our side.

He did, though, have a bit of a habit of doing slightly strange things. In the last game of the 2005 season, with City needing a win to qualify for the UEFA Cup, he decided not to bring on Jon Macken – an actual striker, who was sitting on the bench – for the final few minutes, and sent David James up front. The David James who made his name as a goalkeeper. He even took an outfield player off so that he could put Nicky Weaver, the substitute keeper, on. It didn't work. I don't quite know what the logic of that one was, but Pearce was a big believer in players creating a bit of havoc. He loved havoc, and nothing says havoc quite like your goalkeeper suddenly being used as a striker.

My guess is that he had much the same idea a few months later when we were losing at Highbury and he summoned me from the bench. There were only about five minutes to go, and I was meant to go on and cause chaos. I wasn't going on as a right-back. I wasn't even going on as a central defender. Pearce wanted me to play as a forward. I think he was hoping that, because I was a young player, Arsenal would never have seen me before, so they wouldn't really know what to do. The problem was that I'm not sure I really knew what to do, either. There definitely weren't any detailed tactical instructions. He just told me to get on the pitch and 'have fun'. Thanks, Stuart. Trying to get the better of Sol Campbell? Sounds like a load of fun.

In his defence, I had played as a forward before. The more I developed as a player, the further back the pitch I moved. I was a forward when I joined Oldham, and I was a pretty good one. I scored quite a lot of goals, back in the day. City never thought I'd make it there, so when I moved to the academy they started playing me in midfield. They were clear about that from the start: they explained to me how they planned to make the most of my talent. They only moved me back into defence because of an injury in a Youth Cup game; they kept me there because they thought the responsibility would help me improve. I'd only start playing as a right-back when I made it into the first team, because ultimately nobody really trusts a kid to play at centre-half.

When I came on at Highbury, then, at least I had some sort of idea of what I was supposed to be doing. It didn't quite work. I had one chance: a volley, late on. I used it to prove all of the coaches and scouts at Manchester City right. The ball spun off the outside of my foot and dribbled away to the corner flag. I'm not even sure it crossed the line. We lost the game. Nobody tried to play me as a striker again.

I've never really counted that as my debut. My real debut came later that season, at home to Charlton. I'd not got back into the team after my showing against Arsenal. I was on the bench a couple of times, but it was months later that I finally got a few more minutes in the Premier League under my belt, and I didn't start a game until the middle of February. Even then, I had to get lucky. Or I had to wait for someone else to be unlucky. Danny Mills and Nedum Onuoha were both injured that week. Pearce didn't have any choice, not really. I was next in line. That's how young players get a chance, most of the time. It was the same, years later, for Marcus Rashford, and for Trent Alexander-Arnold. Your opportunity comes because of a crisis. You just have to make sure you take it.

I wasn't perfect, by any stretch of the imagination. It wasn't a dream debut. I was at fault for one of Charlton's goals. It was exactly the sort of mistake that a young player makes, allowing Darren Bent to jump at the back of me at the far post. But we won the game, and mistakes tend to be forgotten if you get away with them.

It was after that game that things felt different. My life outside football changed. There was a real excitement among Manchester City's fans. I saw myself described as the one they'd been waiting for, a genuine, home-grown superstar. I was the real deal, apparently. Some of the older ones were comparing me to Duncan Edwards. Some of the younger ones had decided that I was a Chapeltown Cannavaro, even though I was playing as a right-back, and he was about five months away from lifting the World Cup. People started noticing me in the street. My name was all over the Manchester City forums. I was the talk of the town.

But my life inside football changed, too. The Charlton game was the end of one period of my career and the start of another. There wasn't any danger of me being sent back down to the academy again, of having to split my time, having to prove myself. I was part of the first team, now, and I was treated like it by the rest of the squad. A week later, I scored my first goal in senior football: a last-minute equaliser in an FA Cup game at Villa Park. I had my place, and I wasn't about to give it up. It might have been as a full-back because there was no way I was dislodging Dunne or Distin, but that was fine. I'd never played there before, but I did well enough for Pearce to keep me in the team for most of the rest of the season. By the end of it – although I didn't know it at the time – I'd already attracted the attention of the England manager. Like all of the other young players who had come through the academy, like Shaun Wright-Phillips and Nedum and Stephen Ireland, I wasn't a kid anymore. We were grown-ups. Even if we still didn't quite know how to have a dinner party.

6

ALWAYS READ THE LABEL

The queue was inching forward. There were four people ahead of me. Then there were three. Then two. I could sense the pressure building. I could feel the eyes on me. I started to look for a way out, any way out. Soon, it would be my turn. I'd be at the counter, and I'd have a choice to make.

I would either have to be humiliated in front of all of these people, or I would have to buy a coat that I couldn't afford.

We always looked forward to away games in London, particularly in the first couple of years after I'd broken through at Manchester City. There was always the prospect of a good night out at one of the clubs that catered to the refined taste of footballers in their late teens and early twenties. But for those of us playing at teams in the north, the main appeal was always the shopping.

I don't quite know why that was. If you were playing in Leeds or Liverpool or, most of all, Manchester, you could buy pretty much anything you might want without even having to go on the motorway. Manchester even had a Harvey Nichols. But there was something special about London. Maybe it was because there was so much more choice. Maybe it was because it had a little bit of glamour about it. Maybe it was because that was where Harrods was.

The most embarrassing moment of my life came not long after I'd made that step from City's academy to the first team. We'd travelled down to London for a game against, I think, West Ham, and I'd sneaked out after the team dinner, jumped into a taxi and headed off to do a little bit of late-night shopping. There was a leather jacket in Harrods that I'd had my eye on, and I'd made up my mind that I was going to go and buy it. I was a Premier League footballer now. I'd hit the big time. And that's the sort of thing you do, when you're big time: you go and buy leather jackets in Harrods.

Harrods is full of big hitters. Or, at least, it's full of people who think they're big hitters, people pretending to be big hitters. At that stage, I was probably in that group. I might have been playing in the Premier League, but I wasn't yet on Premier League wages. I was still on the first proper contract I'd signed, worth about £500 a week. That was a lot of money to me, then, but it's not really Harrods money. Still, I'd seen this jacket for £250, and I decided it was worth half a week's wages. Things were going well. I was allowed to treat myself now and again.

The problem started when I was in the queue, waiting to pay. I checked the label again. I'd not read it carefully enough. The jacket wasn't £250. It was £2,500. That was more than a month's wages. More importantly, it was quite a lot more money than I had in my bank account. I knew you could go into your overdraft, but I didn't know what the limit was, and I suspected it probably wasn't £2,500. I didn't have that sort of money to spend on a coat.

But the alternative wasn't much more appealing. I didn't want to get to the counter and have to admit I'd misread the label and that I didn't have two and a half grand to drop on a leather jacket. The whole queue would see. I'd be a laughing stock. They probably wouldn't recognise me – that was one of the benefits of those early days at City, before we became regular contenders for trophies: you could live your life however you wanted, and people didn't pay you the slightest bit of attention – but that didn't matter. They would all see me having to leave Harrods with my tail between my legs. They'd have caught me pretending to be a big shot, when really I was a kid with an HSBC debit card, worrying about my overdraft.

There was only one option. I was going to have to style this out. As I approached the counter, as subtly as I could, I pulled my phone from my pocket. This wouldn't have been an iPhone – they hadn't come out by that stage. This would have been a BlackBerry or a Motorola or a Nokia or something. They all gave you the choice of listening to your ringtones. I opened them up, played one at random, lifted the phone to my ear and pretended to answer.

'What's that? We've got a meeting? Yeah, yeah. I'll be back soon. I'll come back straightaway. Yeah, yeah. Thanks.' I could see the rest of the queue wondering what the holdup might be. I mouthed to the assistant at the counter to hold the jacket for me – I just had to dash off, important footballer business, just keep it to one side and I'd be back later to come and pay for it – and walked out of the shop as quickly as I could. I didn't go back into Harrods for a long time, just in case someone recognised me. That would have been terrible. They might have laughed at the footballer who ran away from a coat. Or worse: they might have made me buy it. I wasn't ready to spend £2,500 on a jacket. I was a long way from being ready to spend £2,500 on a jacket.

At first, the money comes at you slowly in football. When I was at City's academy, I might have been on about £50 a week, plus appearance bonuses and travel expenses. When I turned 16 and signed my first proper professional contract, that went up to £500 a week. To a teenager, especially a teenager that grew up in Chapeltown, that's a ridiculous amount of money. It's all spending money, too, because the club is taking care of your rent and your bills, providing you with training gear and transport, and even cooking some of your meals. That's when you start to think you've made it.

For the lucky few who go even further, though, it's just the beginning. When I made it into the first team at City, they bumped me up to £5,000 a week. That opens up a whole new world to you. It's more money than you ever thought you might see. It's more money than you know what to do with. It's such a leap that it's quite hard to get your head around, but there is more to come. Not long after that, once I'd become a regular, they wanted to improve my deal again. Stuart Pearce burst into the dressing room one day and told me that I was costing him 'an arm and a leg'. He knew an 18-year-old on the verge of becoming an England international was the sort of thing a club had to pay for. That status was the sort of thing that really should be reflected in my contract. He offered me £11,000 a week. That's more than half a million a year. It would have doubled my wages, only a few months after I'd signed the first deal. I was buzzing. I'd have signed happily. I had a great relationship with Stuart and didn't want to do anything that might offend him, but my agent told me to wait. Once I'd made my England debut, not too long after, everything went completely out of proportion. The next deal I signed paid me £50,000 a week. It all happened in the space of two years, or not much more. Once you've made it, the money comes at you thick and fast.

It's not just your contract, either. There are all of the sponsorship deals, too. At academy level, the most talented kids will have contracts with the major sports brands from the age of about 14. Adidas or Nike or Puma or whoever have their own scouts, scouring the country for the best prospects, and they'll lure them in with £10,000 or £20,000 a year, as well as giving them as much kit as they need. They'll always have the best boots, the newest boots. I was expecting to get that sort of deal when I started to play for England's Under-16s, but it never came. Defenders aren't worth as much as flair players to the brands. That's where they committed all of their money. They were the ones who would prove valuable when they turned pro.

Nobody grows up idolising the right-back. Well, maybe Gary Neville, but nobody normal. My agents would try to sort something out for me – I was a hot prospect, after all – but they'd come back and say that they weren't sure about me, they didn't know whether I'd make it, whether I was a good investment. It was only after I turned 18 that I got a proper boot deal, with Adidas. Eventually, they'd even launch my own boot. It was called the Adidas Bling, and it was beautiful: silver and blue and sleek. It did not sell well.

By the time a player is established in the first team at a Premier League club, they have so much money that they can't really make sense of it. Every month, you get a pay slip. It looks like pretty much everyone else's pay slip. There's a pension contribution of about £300 a month. There's your National Insurance contributions. There's the amount that has been taken off in tax. What's different are the figures involved. Throw in bonuses for appearances and goals and clean sheets and victories and all the rest of it, and you'd be clearing £130,000 a month. And you know that is coming to you every month for the next four or five or even six years, no matter what happens. That's not including the signing-on fee, the golden handshake that appears after signing the contract. That could be another five or six – or if you're really good – seven figures.

The first six months after I signed that contract, I decided that I would buy whatever I wanted. As a footballer that meant a few very specific things: jewellery, watches, cars, clothes, holidays. I went to Las Vegas and spent £100,000. I went to Los Angeles and spent £100,000. I bought an Aston Martin and a Range Rover before I turned 20. I splashed out on at least one diamond-encrusted watch. The only thing I didn't end up buying was that leather jacket from Harrods. That was the one that got away.

Those are the things you aspire to have, as a player, because those are the things that everyone is talking about in the dressing room. Players compete with each other on everything, and about money most of all. Who has the best car? Who has the best watch? Who has the biggest house? Everyone is trying to outdo everyone else. Everyone is trying to keep up with the Phil Joneses.

They will even compete with each other over what bank they use. After signing that first contract, I went down to have a meeting at Coutts, the Queen's bank. I didn't know what the difference was between Coutts and the Bradford and Bingley, but it has a clout to it, and players are suckers for clout. A normal bank isn't good enough for football-ers. It has to be the Queen's bank. I made sure I was dressed for the occasion: a smart Dolce & Gabbana blazer, a good pair of trousers, smart shoes. There was a silver Dolce pin that everyone was wearing back then – no idea why, but everyone was doing it, so you did it – so I made sure that was front and centre. And then I went off to the Strand for a presentation on how I could make my money work for me. It was entitled 'Micah Richards: The Non-Footballer', which felt like the sort of thing that fans might say about me after a bad game, but was really about how to build my brand, how to diversify my portfolio, how to make sure the money I was earning then lasted me and my family for generations.

I came out of that with two cards: a Coutts card and a Coutts World, which does all the same things as any other credit card, except you have to have an annual income of more than half a million to get one. It can also, allegedly, get you through queues at airports, but I've never tested that out. I'm not sure what the security staff would make of me flashing a credit card at them. Coutts does carry some weight, though. You get a different level of respect with Coutts. My jeweller, for example, does not take cheques, because he is a jeweller in the twenty-first century, and not the 1890s. But he will take a Coutts cheque, because he knows it's not going to bounce. It's the sort of thing that impresses other players, too. I bounced back into City after that meeting, beaming that the establishment had finally accepted me and thumping my Coutts card down on the table. It didn't last. After a while, having a normal Coutts card wasn't enough. You had to have the black Coutts card. That was the one that really mattered, that showed you were special. It will be something different now. Players can't help but compete with each other.

Most of them, anyway. Not everyone feels compelled to get involved. At City, we had a squad that included both Stephen Ireland and Javi Garrido. Ireland took the competition on watches and jewellery and, in particular, cars extremely seriously. It wasn't enough that he had the right car, the best car, he also had to have it in a colour that nobody else did. His pink Baby Bentley became the stuff of legend. Later on, Mario Balotelli went one step further and got a custom paint job to make his Bentley camouflage. Garrido was at the opposite end of the scale. He had a really nice flat in Hale, a leafy suburb in south Manchester where a lot of the players lived, but he just did not care at all about cars. He didn't think he needed a flash one. He would turn up for training or for games in a Peugeot. It was a perfectly good car, but it looked out of place among the supercars all around it. When he left the Etihad Stadium after games, we would all get stopped by fans looking for autographs. They could tell who the players were because of what they were driving. (Stephen Ireland was not hard to spot.) Then Garrido would trundle out in his Peugeot, nobody even bothering to look at him. They assumed he was staff.

He got battered in training every day for what he drove, but looking back it must have taken an amazing amount of confidence to opt out of that competition, to accept all of the banter and not crumble. For the rest of us, it did not feel optional. Money matters to players. How much you are on is important enough for people to lie about it. Richard Dunne once asked me, when I was first coming through, how much I was earning. I'd been linked to Chelsea, and he had always been honest with me, looked after me; he wasn't being nosy so much as thinking about what was best for my career. I thought about lying to him but going the other way: I was pretty sure I was on more than him, and he was the club captain. I didn't want to create a problem. But I owed him the truth, and he understood: they had to give me that money so that, when it came time to sell me, they got the sort of fee that they were expecting.

Most players go the other way. They'll maybe add an extra few thousand to their wages so that the rest of the dressing room thinks they're more important than they are. Only once you have made it, once you're completely sure of your place, can you be honest. I once saw one of Balotelli's pay slips. It made my eyes pop out of my head. He didn't need to add a bit of sauce to it. The amount City were paying him said everything he needed to say. That's the thing about money in football: it's not just about how much you take home. It's about how much you're valued by the club. Your salary is, quite a lot of the time, your self-esteem. Players will tell you how much they think they should be on, not how much they're on. It is all about keeping your place in the pecking order, about fitting in. It's the same for how you spend that money. You feel like you have to have the cars and the clothes and the watches and the jewellery. You have to live like everyone else. You have to spend your money like a footballer just to be accepted.

It was Andy Cole who snapped me out of that. Andy joined City towards the end of his career, after his glory years with Newcastle and Manchester United. I was just a kid, but we always got along well. He gave me two nicknames. He'd call me 'Topper', because he thought I always got a bit carried away with my tackling and went in too high on the other players. I took particular pleasure in smashing some of the older boys. And he'd call me 'Micah the Hitter', for very similar reasons. Looking back, he may have been trying to tell me something about my physical approach.

One day, when I was still spending money like it was about to run out, I came into training with an all-diamond watch. It had cost me a fortune, and I was keen to show it off. Cole was unimpressed. He came up to me and asked: 'Topper, what do you think you're doing?' I was offended. I was never the sort to back down, even to someone like him, and I didn't like the idea of him having a go at me. I started to argue with him, to tell him not to come to me and criticise, but he didn't rise to it. He just asked me where my parents were living. They were still in their old house in Chapeltown, I said. 'And how much would that house cost?' he said. I didn't know, but I was pretty sure that a watch made entirely from diamonds would make a decent deposit. 'And yet you're buying this,' he said, pointing at the watch. 'If you have enough money, if you've done what you need to do, buy whatever you want,' he said. 'But don't buy all this stuff first when you don't have all the other stuff lined up. Don't fall into that trap.'

I don't think I ever told him, but that speech changed my life. It was a kick up the arse. I don't know why he singled me out for help. Maybe he saw me as a younger version of himself: a young black kid who was going to have to work out what to do with all of the money coming his way. Maybe, despite my sometimes wayward tackling, he'd got a soft spot for me, and he didn't want me to go down that road. Either way, it was a little bit of harsh reality that I needed. I made sure, from that point on, that my future and my family's future was secure. I bought my parents a house. I got myself a financial advisor. I started to invest in property.

Even then, you have to be careful. There are a lot of people out there who see players as easy targets: young men with a lot of money and no real idea what they're doing, ripe to be ripped off. They think that you're not very bright. They're sure that you won't read the small print. Everyone is trying to line their pockets.

Agents will recommend you to certain financial advisors or car dealers or people who can provide you with jewellery or watches or security, and they will often get what's called an 'introduction fee' for their trouble. That's one phrase for it. I'm pretty sure there's another one. The players don't know any different, so they just go along with it, and everyone assumes that you won't notice that you're being fleeced.

Friends – or at least acquaintances – will come out of the woodwork once you have made it, people you haven't seen or spoken to or even thought about in years. It might be someone you grew up with, or someone you played with in the academy. They'll have a business proposal, and they will want a loan to help them get it off the ground. But they're not loans that get paid back, let alone with a bit of interest.

And then, sometimes, there are other players who try to sell you things, who hope that they can use a bit of peer pressure to separate you from some of your money. I think a lot of players in the generation just before mine – the one that included the golden generation – took advantage of that. I don't know whether they were more susceptible to these schemes, or whether they had an attitude that they had to make as much money as they could because they started at a time when wages were not quite as high as they are now, but either way it felt some of them always had something to sell.

It might have been timeshares in Dubai, or they might have been put on to a property scheme in Tunisia. They might have a legitimate interest in it. They might truly believe it is a genuine opportunity. They might just be a frontman, getting a deal in exchange for bringing other players on board. That can work, especially if it is coming from a senior player, someone that the rest of a squad, for club or country, looks up to: a player who seems to have sorted out their own finances. If they're recommending something, you're much more likely to listen. If this has worked for him, maybe it will work for me. They might tell you it's a great opportunity and you can't afford to miss it. They might just hope that knowing that everyone else is involved will be enough to tempt you. Or they'll rely on the fact that a lot of players don't really care. They'll be willing to take a bit of a risk on some vague property deal because they know that, even if it doesn't work out, there's another £200,000 coming their way next month, or the next month after that. You can spend what you want, and there won't be any consequences.

Or so you think, anyway. I know lots of players who would have been earning eye-watering sums of money at the peaks of their careers – £50,000 a week, £75,000 a week, £100,000 a week – but have nothing now. I understand that a lot of people will find it hard to have any sympathy at all for them. The assumption will be that they had the chance to make more money in a couple of years than some people will see in a lifetime and they wasted it all on cars and watches and leather jackets in Harrods. You can't really feel sorry for someone who changed their car every six months just to make sure they were winning some ridiculous competition with their teammates, rather than thought about what might happen after they retire.

The reality is more complicated than that. Of course, some players do fritter their money away. Others find it hard to get used to what life is like when that money has stopped coming in, when they come to the end of their contracts and those pay slips no longer appear. Your outgoings tend to match your income. If you're on £50,000 a month after tax, you will have a lifestyle that reflects that. Your wife or your girlfriend might be used to it. It's hard to change that in those first few years after retirement, to get used to a slightly less glamorous sort of existence. Most of the time, there is nobody to guide you through that change. A club might put you in touch with a financial advisor, and they might help. But most agents don't take much interest in setting their clients up for life after football; even now there is plenty of research to show just how many players struggle with bankruptcy and divorce and addiction once their careers have ended.

The biggest issue, though, is family. The wages of a single player will often support not just their immediate family – their mum and dad, their brothers and sisters, their partner and children – but an extended family, too.

You want to do it, of course, you want to help everyone who helped you when you were younger, but you also feel obliged to do it. You feel like you don't have any choice. It is up to you to look after everyone. And when you're doing that, the money does not go quite as far as you think it will. Without proper planning, it can disappear pretty quickly.

It is why I try not to accuse players of being interested in nothing but money. Of course that is why some players move to certain clubs. Robinho did not join Manchester City, the signing that started the club's new era, because he grew up watching videos of Georgi Kinkladze. He was not determined to end the supremacy of Manchester United. He wasn't excited by the project. He did it for the dough. Obviously he did it for the dough. But then he probably knew that he had a short career, and dozens of people who were reliant on him in Brazil. He had to maximise his earnings. He had to make sure as many of them got as much as possible.

It was the same for one of his international teammates. I played against Oscar when he was at Chelsea. He was quick, smart, inventive. He was class. He could have spent a decade in the Premier League, and he would have won a handful of titles, too. But instead, at the age of 24, he went to China. He must have really loved China. I bet when he was playing in England, his teammates were sick of him talking about China, how much he wanted to live there, how much he dreamed of moving to Shanghai. I'm sure he didn't go for the money at all. I'm sure the £60 million or whatever that he's earning since he went there didn't make the slightest bit of difference to him. He just really loved China.

As easy as it would be to criticise, to say that he wasted his career and his talent, I can see why he did it. He went because someone was daft enough to pay him tens of millions of pounds, the sort of money that could change the course of his family's life forever. It will be enough to look after not just this generation, but the next two or three, too, maybe more. Ultimately, football is a job. That is made perfectly clear to you by clubs and managers and even fans, at times. It's his right to treat it as one, to make sure that it works for him.

Money does matter to players. How much they earn is a way of seeing how much they are worth. That there is so much pressure to spend it on certain things is really just a way of showing that you belong, that you are valued. Players judge themselves by how much they earn because that is how clubs and fans judge them, too. But it was not players who made football about money. We were all playing as kids. We played for nothing, and then as academy kids, we devoted our lives to something for next to nothing. It was everyone else – the broadcasters and the media and the leagues and the governing bodies – who did all they could to bring as much money in as possible, to pump football full of money, to make it all about money. Football thinks constantly about money. All players are doing is taking the same approach.

7

KICKING SANDWICHES AT ROBERTO MANCINI

Something had changed. You knew it as soon as you drove into Carrington, Manchester City's training ground, even if you didn't quite know what it was. It took a moment to put your finger on it. The skyline. Those poles, the ones rising higher and higher above the pitch where the first team trained, they weren't there yesterday. What were they? They looked like floodlights. Why would they be installing floodlights above the training pitches?

It had been a strange few days. Things had changed at City in the blink of an eye. Mark Hughes had been sacked as manager a week or so before Christmas 2009. It was announced a couple of hours after we'd beaten Sunderland 4–3 at the Etihad, but really the decision had been made long before that. Hughes seemed to know something was coming. When the final whistle blew, he made a point of walking to every corner of the stadium, applauding the crowd. When we got into the dressing room, he gathered all of the players together and told us that he didn't know for certain, but it looked like he might be about to get sacked.

Then he walked out of the room and left us to it. Life for managers is even less sentimental than it is for players.

I wasn't necessarily devastated that he'd gone. Hughes was a lovely person, a really nice guy, and a great attacking coach. He loved me as a player, too. I think I played more games in a season under him than I did under any other manager. But I never really felt as though I was learning a vast amount from him. He didn't improve me as a defender. I don't think he quite knew how to get the best out of me. That's not just down to him. It's down to me, too. Maybe I wasn't as willing to learn at that stage in my career as I should have been.

There was a bit of a personality clash with his staff, too. Hughes came as a package: he brought Eddie Niedzwiecki with him as a first-team coach, and Mark Bowen as his assistant. Eddie was brilliant. Players loved him. His sessions were inventive and engaging and fun, just like training should be. Bowen was there as the bad cop, Hughes's pitbull, snapping and snarling and keeping everyone in line. I didn't take especially well to that.

The day after one game, a defeat, Bowen accused me of laughing as we were on the pitch, going through all of the things we'd done wrong. At first, I wasn't quite sure who he was talking to, but then I noticed he was looking at me. 'Yeah, fucking you,' he said. I told him I wasn't laughing. He said I was. It felt like he was just trying to take his disappointment at losing a game out on someone, and that someone was me. I didn't like being made a scapegoat, so I told him that all of this was being filmed. There were cameras everywhere. 'Get the film that shows me laughing and you can fine me whatever you want,' I said. The next day, I went to see Hughes. I was expecting a row. I thought he'd fine me or drop me for standing up to his henchman. Instead, he melted. He was nice as pie to me. There was no punishment, and not just because I hadn't been laughing. Hughes couldn't handle confrontation. He avoided it at all costs. That's why he had Bowen. He did all of the dirty work.

Still, as a player, you know that a change of manager is risky. Your first instinct is always to wonder what it will mean for you. What if the new manager doesn't like me? What if he has a plan for the team that doesn't involve a marauding right-back? What if he hasn't heard of me? Or worse: what if he has heard of me, seen me play, done his research, and decided that I'm terrible? I was pretty sure of my place at Manchester City at that stage. I was home-grown. I was an England international. I was one of the best players at the club. I knew my own worth. I was fear-less. But it's still a delicate moment. A new manager means new ideas. It means proving yourself all over again. It means building a relationship, establishing trust, working out what you can get away with.

The club had known exactly who was going to replace Hughes. Roberto Mancini had won three Serie A titles as manager of Inter Milan before being dismissed to make room for José Mourinho, and City had him lined up to take over without missing a beat. I'm not even sure Hughes had left the building before Mancini was moving his orna-ments into his office. He did not take long to make his presence felt. That is what the floodlights were about.

Once you've made the first team, you get used to a certain rhythm of life. You arrive at the training ground for 10 a.m. or so, maybe earlier if you want to do a bit of gym work or some pre-activation – getting the muscles nice and warm before the warm-up. You train for a couple of hours. Then maybe you have a rub or an ice bath, and probably a bite to eat. Worst-case scenario, you're heading home by 2 p.m. Being an athlete takes over your whole life. You have to eat well. You have to look after your body. You have to be right physically and mentally. It's a lifestyle. But in terms of actual time in the office, the working day is just your typical 10 a.m. to 2 p.m.

The first thing Mancini did was put an end to that. As soon as we got inside the training ground, we had a meeting in one of the physio's rooms. The players were desperate to know what the floodlights were for. It could have been something to do with the reserves or the academy. Maybe they had a game that evening. Or that afternoon, actually: it was Manchester in December. We were working with about three hours of sunlight. Maybe it was the goalkeepers. They sometimes stay later, doing extra work after training, and as a rule it helps if they can see the ball.

The answer was none of the above. Mancini was going to make us do double sessions. Not a double session, today, but double sessions for the foreseeable. That's something you're meant to leave behind when you come out of the academy. Kids train twice a day, once in the morning, once in the afternoon. Hopefuls train twice a day. It's one of the best things about being a professional.

All of a sudden, work seems a bit like a doddle. Except under Roberto Mancini. We'd be doing one session in the morning, hanging around for ages, and then starting another one – under the floodlights – at 4 p.m. It was like sending us back to school. And we'd be working exclusively on team shape. It was cold, it was dark and it was dingy, and now we'd be standing around in formation, learning what runs he wanted us to make.

Mancini felt that we had plenty of talent as individuals, that as players we were unbelievable, but that we basically had no tactics whatsoever as a team. He was going to drill us again and again until he'd changed that.

The reaction was not, it's probably fair to say, overwhelmingly positive. Heads were exploding left, right and centre. Players were shouting and swearing, effing and jeffing. I've never seen a group of highly paid professional athletes transform into a load of whining babies so quickly as the day Roberto Mancini told us that we were going to have to work up to six hours a day.

What a manager needs more than anything else, more than charisma or a philosophy or an impressive playing career, is power. As long as they have power, they will take the players with them. As soon as the dressing room starts to sense that their power is waning, it's over. You can't get that back. Mancini knew he could risk upsetting us all, right from the start, because he had that power. He was the owners' appointment. He was their guy. He was the one they wanted. If there was a power struggle, he would win. We knew he would win. And, most important of all, he knew that we knew he would win. If he wanted us to train in the dark, we'd train in the dark. Anyone who didn't want to train in the dark would be sold. He told us as much. 'If you want stay, stay,' he'd say to us, quite a lot. 'If you want go, go.' He didn't care. That was the source of his authority. Those floodlights were a message. You were either with him, or against him.

At a club like Manchester City at that time, that was crucial. When Mancini arrived, in 2009, the squad had been totally transformed by the money the owners had poured in. The team was full of top-class players, and that made it infinitely more difficult to manage. The better the players, remember, the bigger the characters. It wasn't just Vincent Kompany, the head boy. Vincent would have been a dream for a manager. It was people like Carlos Tevez, the Don Corleone of the dressing room, who didn't care who you were if you upset him. There was Emmanuel Adebayor and Robinho and Craig Bellamy, the man who could make Gareth Barry angry, and within a year or two he would have added Yaya Touré, Mario Balotelli and Samir Nasri to the mix. These were major players. They were used to being the big dog. It could have been a free-for-all. They needed a strong manager to have any chance of controlling them. They needed to know that, however much they cost and however high their reputations and however influential they might be, the ultimate power was somewhere else.

Mancini was perfect for that. Mancini didn't care who he upset. He knew that his word was final with the owners. If he thought a player wasn't good enough, they'd be gone. If he thought a player was too much of a problem, out the door. He didn't mess about. He didn't pull any punches. He ranted and raved and he told anyone and everyone to fuck off when he felt like it. He'd throw his arms around. He'd do it in training. He'd do it before games. He'd do it after games.

As a full-back, he did it constantly during games, too. There was one Premier League match, at Wigan, where I'd chosen the wrong boots. I tended to warm up in moulded studs, just to get a feel for the pitch, and then switch into half-studs for the game itself. But that day the pitch was so dry that I decided that the moulds were the better bet. It was a bad idea. For the first few minutes, I kept slipping over. The one thing Mancini always wanted from me was to stay wide, to get as close to the touchline as possible. That way, David Silva or Samir Nasri or whoever could drop into a pocket, pick up the ball, and I'd be in a position to fly up the wing. I couldn't do it, though, if I was on the ground, struggling to stand up.

All I heard for the first few minutes was Mancini, in the technical area, bellowing: 'Why not wide? Micah, why not wide?' After a while, he'd had enough. He waited until the ball was out of play and summoned me over. 'You have five minutes,' he said. 'If you don't sort yourself out in five minutes, I'm taking you off.'

I only ever saw Mancini back down once. Most managers make sure they have the last word in any argument. Mancini definitely made sure he had the last word in an argument. But a couple of days before the Manchester derby in 2011, he had a falling out with Nasri. It was the biggest argument I had ever seen, and it had started because we were doing his beloved shape work. Mancini had set out the team he wanted to play at Old Trafford, and we were going through the motions of what we'd do in certain situations. We'd shuffle here when they had the ball, run there when we got it back, that sort of thing. Shape work is boring, but it's one of those things you have to do.

After a while, though, Samir's patience snapped. Mancini kept stopping us to move Nasri around. 'No, you here, you here,' he'd say, and then we'd start again. Then a whistle. 'Samir, you here, you here.' Again and again and again until Nasri had enough. 'I know what I'm fucking doing,' he shouted at Mancini, and then he walked off the field. That's a taboo, walking out of a training session, but Nasri wasn't the sort to care. He was not to be messed with. He kept going until he'd disappeared inside.

Mancini started the session again, replaced Nasri with James Milner, and we kept on doing shape work. When we were finished, I headed to the physio room. Nasri was there. Then Mancini came in. They picked up where they'd left off. They were screaming at each other, swearing in French, neither one budging. It was absolute carnage. Eventually, Nasri offered him out. 'Talk to me like that again and I'll kick the shit out of you,' he said. To his manager. I don't think it was an empty threat. Samir wasn't one to back down, either.

Mancini could see, I think, that it was all going too far, and that Nasri wasn't about to defuse the situation. It was the only time I ever saw Mancini walk away. He knew he had to, because otherwise things might have escalated to a point where nobody came out of it well. That weekend, we went to Old Trafford and won 6–1. Milner was brilliant that day. It was maybe the best I ever saw him play. But he wasn't meant to be in the team. Nasri was. Instead he ended up as a sub, punishment for threatening to spark his manager.

For all that he could be just a little unpredictable, I loved working with Mancini. We didn't take to each other immediately. There was one argument we had, during a game in Russia, where I threatened to punch him. We'd conceded a soft goal because Vincent Kompany had missed a header, and a player had sneaked round the back of me to tap home. When we got into the dressing room, Mancini came for me. He'd decided the goal was my fault. It felt to me like it was much easier for him to blame me than it was for him to blame Kompany, his captain, who had actually made the mistake. That wasn't like him: his great strength was that he wasn't bothered by who he had to criticise. So I went straight back at him. That just turned the heat up. He got personal. He started shouting: 'Fuck your mother, fuck your mother.' That was too much for me. I went ballistic. There was a tray of sandwiches for the players to eat after the game, and I started booting them around the room. I don't know if you've ever kicked a sandwich, but it's not actually that satisfying. It's definitely not the best use for a sandwich. I wasn't thinking straight, I was so angry. That was when I decided that kicking the manager, or at least threatening to, would be a much better idea.

But he was the one who really taught me how to defend. That stereotype about Italy being the home of defending is true. Mancini showed me things that, even after all those years in the academy, learning my craft, nobody had ever mentioned. We'd spend hours watching videos, him pointing out the right cues for me to switch from defence to attack. His mantra was always that when I chose to go, I had to go all out. You couldn't hesitate. You couldn't second guess yourself. You either went or you didn't. And when you did, you had to trust that one of your teammates would notice and fill in for you. It took a while, I won him over. Even when the injuries started to mount up, he never lost patience with me. I remember him calling me over in a hotel once and asking me why I'd been ruled out of yet another game. He wasn't angry, that time. He was disappointed, and a little frustrated, but more than anything he seemed quite sad. I told him what the problem was, and he looked me in the eye and said: 'Do you want me to buy another right-back?'

I didn't, of course, but I also didn't want him to think that I was losing confidence in myself. I didn't want him to think that I was too injury-prone to be worth waiting for. 'Whoever you buy, they won't do what I do,' I said. It was meant to be a little assertive, a way of telling him that he should stick with me, that I'd be back to my best, to full fitness, soon. He just looked at me, shook his head, and said: 'I know.'

Obviously, it's the player who is ultimately responsible for how their career turns out. There are some factors that you can't control, of course. A bad injury, or an injury at a bad time, can have a massive impact. So can getting bad advice, or not taking your work seriously enough, or letting it all go to your head. But the managers you encounter are incredibly important, too. They can be the difference between fulfilling your potential or going down as a missed opportunity.

It goes without saying that the better the coaches you have, the more likely you are to get the best out of yourself. It would be a privilege for anyone to work with Pep Guardiola or Jürgen Klopp or Thomas Tuchel. They polish players. They take raw material and turn it into something special. But it's not just a matter of working with the best coach. What makes the difference, more than anything, is finding the right one.

Mancini was the right manager for me, at the right time for me. The way he was just happened to be exactly what I needed at that stage in my career. He had a clear idea for what he wanted me to be. He believed in me. He was willing to teach me. The same approach wouldn't work for everyone. The same approach didn't work for everyone. There were plenty of players who didn't find it nearly so satisfying working with him as I did. But we clicked. We had a genuine bond. We're still in touch now. He meant a lot to me, and I think I meant a lot to him. I was lucky to get the chance to work with him.

I can't say the same for Fabio Capello. By the time he got the England job, his pedigree was unbelievable. He'd managed that great AC Milan team. He'd won the Italian title with Roma. He'd been in charge of Real Madrid. He'd coached Francesco Totti and Gabriel Batistuta and Marco van Basten and Paolo Maldini. Nobody could hold a candle to him, even Mancini. He was more than a superstar. He was a legend. But being the best manager doesn't make you the right manager.

My first coach with England, Steve McClaren, was great. That's the right word for him: he was a coach, more than a manager. He put on sessions that the players loved. You felt you were learning something. He was supportive. He was encouraging. He was nice. You looked forward to being called up by him.

I had a more complicated relationship with Roy Hodgson. The thing I valued most in a manager was honesty. There are a lot of people in football who will tell you what you want to hear. Having someone who will tell you what they really think is crucial. Players appreciate it. They like to know where they stand.

Hodgson disappointed me. He had taken over as England manager just before Euro 2012. I should have been a strong contender to make that squad, to go to my first major tournament for my country. I'd not been picked for the World Cup two years previously, and the whole country had missed out in 2008. I was the starting full-back for the team that was about to win the Premier League title. I was playing the best football of my career.

But there was competition. Kyle Walker was coming through at Tottenham, and would have been first choice had he not picked up an injury a few weeks before the squad was due to be announced. In his absence, Glen Johnson, at Liverpool, would take one of the slots. He was a shoo-in. Manchester United's Phil Jones was so versatile that he might be able to fill in anywhere across the back.

And there was a kid called Martin Kelly who was coming through at Liverpool – though he would go on to spend most of his career at Crystal Palace – who Hodgson liked, too.

In the end, he decided to take Glen and Phil. It was hard not to feel a bit insulted, when Stuart Pearce called to tell me that I wouldn't be going, given that it meant England would be going to the finals with just one specialist right-back. The fact it was Stuart on the phone upset me, too. Roy had obviously decided to get him to deliver the bad news because he knew I had a good relationship with him: he'd been my manager at City. Like Mark Hughes, Roy ducked the confrontation. It felt a little bit cowardly, and it meant I wasn't in the best frame of mind when Stuart asked if I wanted to be on standby in case someone dropped out. It didn't sound especially appealing, waiting around to see if someone got injured so I could go to a tournament and, most likely, not play. When Stuart told me he was taking the Olympic team that summer, and suggested he'd like me to be part of it, that made my mind up. I'd miss the Euros, but the Olympics would more than make up for it. Martin Kelly went on standby instead, and sure enough got the call up to the squad. He played once for England. As a substitute. For two minutes. It's the shortest England career in history.

As much as I resented Roy, he was a dream compared with Capello. I could not stand working with Capello. I hated it, in fact. With Capello, I'd dread getting a call-up. I'd dread going away with England. I'd dread every single training session. When he left me out of the squad for the

2010 World Cup, it still hurt, obviously. It would have been a dream to play for England at a World Cup, but I knew I'd not played especially well that season. But as well as being disappointed, there was part of me that was relieved, too. At least this way I didn't have to spend a month holed up outside Rustenburg with him.

It wasn't that he was old school. It was that he was ancient. He was like a headmaster, but a horrible one, one who took pleasure in making your life a misery. He was another who banned ketchup. Worse than that, he banned all food between lunchtime and dinner. You weren't allowed to snack on anything, except maybe an apple. Complaining about this might sound greedy, but bear in mind it was after training. We'd all just burned a few thousand calories. It was hardly a surprise that we might get peckish. And it's not like anyone was ordering burgers. We just fancied a bit of toast. But no, nothing. At mealtimes, he'd wander around the room, checking on what everyone was eating. These were some of the best players in the world. They knew what they were doing. They didn't need someone checking how much pasta they were having.

Much worse was the way he coached. He made a point of trying to embarrass players during training, stopping a session so that he could slaughter you in front of everyone.

With me, it was always about how I crossed the ball. I won't pretend that I had the technique of David Beckham, or Trent Alexander-Arnold, or David Bentley. But that's because I was a different sort of player. A faster player. They developed that technique because they slowed down before they delivered a cross. Watch Trent play now, and that's what he does. He takes an extra touch, and then whips the ball in.

That wasn't what I did. It isn't what any really quick player does. Your speed is your advantage, so you learn to maximise it. You don't slow down before delivering. You do it at full pelt, and that means you have to deliver it in a certain way. I worked and worked at getting to the byline and then fizzing the ball, low, across the box. I learned to look up, set myself and work out where I was going to hit it, all while I was sprinting. Players like Kyle Walker and Aaron Lennon do exactly the same thing.

Capello, though, didn't want me to do that. He wanted me to slow down, take a touch. That's fine – he's the manager, you do as you're told – but it was the way he chose to tell me. He wouldn't blow his whistle. He would scream the word 'Stop!' at the top of his voice. He'd stride over, get right in my face, and shout at me to 'look up, stop, cross'. He did that with a lot of us. Mancini was tough, but he'd explain that it was for your own good. He wanted you to get better. Capello seemed to be horrible for the sake of it. He acted like you were beneath him.

He was the only manager who ever made me feel like that. That's not to say the others I worked with were perfect, but I'm pretty confident that none of them could ever have questioned my professionalism. I made mistakes during my career. There were times when I wasn't as dedicated to football as I should have been, or as I needed to be. But I was on time for training. I never shirked. I never downed tools. I always showed my teammates and my manager respect, because that's what they deserved.

I liked some more than others, obviously. I'll always be grateful to Stuart Pearce, the man who gave me my debut. Pearce wasn't quite the person you might think from his reputation. Obviously, he was hard. You don't get the nickname 'Psycho' if you're not, well, a bit of a psycho. But he was also kind, and patient, and understanding, or at least he was with me and the rest of the young players that he helped blood at Manchester City.

Sven-Göran Eriksson didn't have Pearce's fiery streak. He was much calmer, much more relaxed, but when he arrived at City he had a natural authority. Sven's reputation has suffered a lot in the last few years, but people forget the career he had. He'd managed Lazio and Benfica and all these massive teams. He'd taken England to a World Cup quarter-final. And he'd had an extremely nice time doing it. He was very charming, Sven. He had a magnetism.

His great strength was his experience. When he arrived, we had a bit of a dilemma. The club had too many good goalkeepers. Kasper Schmeichel had come through the academy with us. He was a very confident kid, Kasper. He would always be the first to have a new gadget, the one showing off whatever piece of technology he had that week. The first person I ever saw with an iPod? Kasper Schmeichel. He always had something to say, too, but he was an extremely talented goalkeeper. But then so was one of his rivals, Joe Hart. Joe had been signed from Shrewsbury Town, and probably hadn't expected to play especially quickly when he arrived. But you could immediately see how good he was: tall and commanding and with brilliant reflexes. There was a case to be made for him. And then there was Andreas Isaksson, a Swedish goalkeeper, and the oldest of the three. He'd been signed as first choice.

There has to be a first-choice goalkeeper. If you keep changing, then the defence is always just a little bit unsettled. Different keepers have different ways of playing. You need to know, as a centre-half, when they're going to come for a cross and when they'll stay on their line. You need to have that bond with them. That's impossible to build if it's a different person standing behind you every week.

Eriksson's solution led to what may have been the most awkward moment of my career. He called me and Richard Dunne into his office one day. It made sense: Dunne was the captain, and together me and him were the first-choice central defenders. He needed to know who we wanted to be the goalkeeper, who we were most comfortable with. Richard was old enough to have been used to that sort of thing. It was part of his job. It was different for me. I was 19, and he was basically asking me to knife one of my mates. I'd grown up with Kasper. I was close to Joe. I didn't know Andreas all that well, but I'm sure he was nice, too. I didn't know what to say. I didn't really want to say anything. For the first time in my life, I felt like I was being sly. It's lucky, really, that both went on to have such brilliant careers. They've both won the Premier League and the FA Cup. They've both played multiple times for their countries. They've both been outstanding goalkeepers. Nobody needs to know that me and Richard Dunne told Sven to play Joe, and not Kasper.

As difficult as that was, it was a good piece of management. Sven needed his centre-halves to feel comfortable. He needed us to feel empowered. That was how he went about his job. In a way, that was his downfall. At times, he farmed out too much of the responsibility. He was just a bit too passive. In his last game in charge of the single season he had at City, we lost 8–1 at Middlesbrough. It was a complete humiliation. Players are expecting to get the full force of their manager's anger then. It's the time for the manager to stamp their authority on the squad. But Sven was standing on the touchline, not really doing much. He should have been prowling up and down, telling everyone exactly what he thought of them. Instead, he just seemed to be watching it all unfold.

It's important to have boundaries with a manager. I learned that with Manuel Pellegrini, my final manager at Manchester City, and for a while my potential tenant. I had a house in Manchester that I'd rented out to a succession of players, some from City, some from other teams. I'd never had any problems. Well, apart from the one player who had the bailiffs come round after forgetting to pay all of his bills, anyway. Danilo lived there for a while. So did David Silva. Samir Nasri tried to rent it, too, offering me way over the asking price, but I had to turn him down because we'd already signed a contract with David. There was no better tenant than Memphis Depay, though. He left Manchester United in the middle of his second season, but he didn't have enough warning that the move was coming to give me the six months' notice he needed to cancel his contract. It meant that I could wait for him to move all of his stuff to Lyon, and rent it out again. A nice bit of double bubble for me.

That list of my former tenants almost included Pellegrini. He had come to look round the house when he first moved to Manchester. He was an engineer by training, and he was fascinated by the architecture. We did a little tour, and I could tell he was quite taken with it. He said he'd come back to me, and sure enough, he texted me a little while later with an offer. I was suddenly a little bit unsure about the idea, though. What if something went wrong? Would he drop me because I hadn't sorted out a patch of damp quickly enough? Would people think I was only in the team because I'd given him a cut-price rate? It would be weird acting as the landlord to my boss. The whole thing started to stress me out. He kept texting, asking about the house, when it would be available. I didn't know what to say. Eventually, I had to pretend that I'd decided to live there myself, just to put an end to it all. He didn't seem to hold it against me. Though I wasn't as close to him as I was to Mancini, I had a great relationship with Pellegrini. He was the man who told me I had to leave Manchester City, of course, but he handled it with dignity and with class. I always respected him.

Even when I had a manager who I found it a little harder to admire, I didn't drop my standards. Tim Sherwood had taken me to Aston Villa. He was tactically sharp, he knew how to build a team spirit, he knew how to talk to players. He didn't sugarcoat anything. He let me know what he needed me to do, and I responded to that. There may not be a lot of Villa fans who remember it, but in those first few months at Villa Park, I was playing really well. There was a suggestion that I might force my way back into the England squad. That was because of Sherwood. I loved working with him.

It was when he was replaced by Rémi Garde that everything started to go wrong. I hadn't had a problem with his appointment: he'd been at Lyon for three years as a coach, and he'd played under Arsène Wenger at Arsenal, so he came with a decent reputation. My only concern was whether or not he spoke English. We had quite a few French, or French-speaking, players in the squad, and I didn't want a divide to develop. That was something Sherwood had been really good at avoiding, and it's the sort of thing that can kill a team, especially one trying to avoid relegation. I mentioned my worry to someone at the club, and they obviously passed it on to him. On one of his first days, he pulled me aside to reassure me. Everything would be in English, he said. He didn't want a divide either. He wanted me to be his leader. It was all cool. There was no problem.

Or at least there wasn't until he introduced us to his fitness coach. One of the first sessions he did had us clambering over an obstacle course. That would be bad in pre-season, but to do it in the middle of a campaign, when players are nursing all sorts of knocks and injuries, was asking for trouble. I could feel my knee swelling up as I did it. They weren't willing to listen when we suggested it wasn't going down well with the squad. They were trying to impose themselves, but they lacked the authority to do it. Garde wasn't as strong as Mancini. He didn't have the absolute backing of the owners. He was in a desperate situation, and he was trying to save his own career, too. The players could sense that.

There was worse to come. The training sessions they ran were not so much back to basics as back in time. His staff would ask a group of Premier League footballers to do the simplest five-yard passing drills, as if they were teaching a load of children how to play football. We would be told not to dribble the ball without stopping it first. They were sessions from some basic training manual, one that would have been out of date years beforehand. That was not a great Aston Villa team, by any means. But it wasn't quite that bad. We knew how to pass a football, even if it wasn't always immediately apparent during games.

Garde's biggest mistake, though, was alienating his single most important player. He might have wanted me to be his leader, but Gabby Agbonlahor was the heart of the club. He was the central character in that dressing room. He was a Villa fan. He'd been there for his entire career. The fans adored him. He was the guy who set the tone of the dressing room. The mood of the squad depended on how he was feeling. He was the one player that any manager would need onside if they were to be a success. Garde didn't manage to do that. Him and Gabby were oil and water.

Some players are all or nothing. If you give them the power they need, the power they want, you'll get the best out of them. Something similar happened – though maybe with just a slightly better player than Gabby – when Cristiano Ronaldo went back to Manchester United. He needs to be the main man. Everything has to be built around him. If it is, he'll be happy, and he'll perform for you. If he's not, if the manager isn't willing to do that, then there's no point having him around. You don't really have a choice but to sell him.

The problem for Garde was that he didn't do either. He didn't empower Gabby, but he couldn't get rid of him. That led to an awkward stand-off. Gabby was still there at the club, he just wasn't playing. The atmosphere turned toxic. The dressing room is meant to be a sanctuary. You're all meant to be united. Instead, Garde had broken it into factions. There are a lot of sheep in any dressing room, people who will align themselves with whoever is the most powerful, and it was significant that Gabby had more allies than Garde did. It was over for him from that moment. Not because he was busy not playing one of his most dangerous players, but because he no longer had the power. And that, above anything else, is what a manager needs to survive.

Mancini could put the floodlights in at the start because he had it. He could tell the players that we would be sold if we didn't submit to his authority because the owners backed him. He could shout and scream at us all he liked. Well, all of us except for Samir Nasri. He had the power to do that. Once it started to wane, though, once results turned and his place wasn't quite as secure, once it looked like maybe he wasn't the owners' man anymore, it was only going to end one way. Something had changed again, in the blink of an eye.

8

SOMEONE ELSE'S SHOES

This was not a good start. I was standing in my room in The Grove, the country house-style hotel just outside London where England used to gather before games at Wembley, and I had a major problem. At the age of 18, I'd been called up to the national team for the first time. I was due downstairs for training in just a few minutes. The whole of the golden generation would be there: Wayne Rooney, Steven Gerrard, Rio Ferdinand, John Terry, David Beckham. It was my chance to prove that I belonged in that company, to show that I was the coming force, the new sensation. And now it appeared that I'd have to do it with two left feet.

Most of the time, the fact that you, as a player, don't have to think about anything other than football is a massive advantage. You can focus exclusively on being at your best on the pitch. All of the other stuff, the boring stuff, is taken care of by someone else. That includes, I learned after I was first told I'd made it into the England squad, packing your kitbag for international duty. It makes sense, I suppose. A footballer can't be expected to remember that they should probably take some boots with them.

That meant it was down to Les Chapman – the man everyone called Chappy – to make sure I had everything I needed for my first appearance with England. Chappy was a legend at Manchester City. He was an institution. The players and the staff loved him. He looked after everyone and everything. I feel bad pointing the finger at him, and not just because really I should have simply sorted my things out myself, but he let me down that day.

Just before I went downstairs, I'd gone into my bag and grabbed the pair of boots he'd put in for me. The problem was that they were both left boots. That's not ideal. First impressions matter in football, both to players and to managers. Fail to prepare, prepare to fail and all that. Now, I was going to have to go downstairs and tell Steve McClaren, the man who'd given me my England chance, and some of the most famous players in the world, some of the best players in the world, that I'd forgotten my boots.

I had no idea what to do. I poked my head out of the door, to see if there was a friendly face around, someone who might help out. And just at that moment, Steven Gerrard walked past. I didn't know Steven Gerrard at all. I'd played against him a few times, and I'd always been in awe of him. You'd see him in the tunnel at Anfield and it was impossible not to be intimidated. He had an aura. A furrowed brow. A silent stare. He'd go out on the pitch, and he'd boss everything. He'd land the first tackle. He'd set the tempo. He'd dominate the referee. Normally, he'd end up winning. I hated playing at Anfield. Anfield, and Steven Gerrard, brought me nothing but misery.

Still, he was my only hope. I sidled up to him with a sheepish grin on my face. I must have seemed like a nervous schoolboy. I told him what had happened. The kitman had put two left boots in my bag, and now I didn't know what to do. It was a risk, but there was no other option. 'I don't suppose you've got a pair I could borrow?'

The thing I learned about Steven Gerrard, in the corridor at The Grove, is that he's one of the nicest people you'll meet. The seriousness only started when he crossed the touchline. Then, he was in his zone. He was doing his thing and he wasn't messing around. The rest of the time, he was humble and open and sound. He was diamond. He had banter. He was by far the best character in that England dressing room. He smiled at me and said no problem. He'd be happy to help me out. He nipped back to his room, grabbed a spare pair of Predators, and threw them to me. I couldn't thank him enough.

I'm not sure I've ever had a better training session than the one that followed. I was like a different player. The boots weren't even the right size for me, but I was spraying cross-field passes, pinging them to everyone. I was crunching into tackles. I was doing skills, skipping past people for fun. It was like I was channelling him. It was hard not to think that maybe Steven Gerrard's secret was that he was just a normal boy transformed into a superstar by a pair of magic boots, like in a comic. That's definitely more likely than me being so relieved not to embarrass myself, and so distracted by his kindness, that all of the stress and pressure of training with England just evaporated, and I could just do my thing.

That was not the effect that England had on everyone. Most of the time, I was the only Manchester City player in the squad. It wasn't like now, when there are half a dozen City players all travelling down together. I was ahead of my time like that. I had to get a car down on my own. I had to figure out how everything worked by myself.

Fortunately, even as an 18-year-old, I wasn't fazed by much. I might have got nervous asking one of Liverpool's greatest ever players if he had a spare pair of boots, but apart from that, I had the fearlessness of youth. It felt natural to be called up for England. I felt like I deserved to be there. I felt like I belonged. I was occasionally a little bit starstruck, but only in certain circumstances: meeting David Beckham for the first time, in particular, I didn't quite know what to say.

That might have been different if my England career had started even earlier. Nobody at Manchester City ever mentioned it to me at the time – I suspect they thought it might be a distraction, or that it might feed my ego just a little bit too much – but Sven-Göran Eriksson had sent some of his staff to watch me at Manchester City before the 2006 World Cup. He wanted to take a young player not as an active member of the squad, but to get a bit of experience of what it is like being at a major tournament. That I wasn't even playing that regularly for City at the time did not seem to matter. I'd only ever played a handful of senior games at that point, and even fewer as a right-back, but he still thought I fitted the bill. He thought about it, but eventually decided to take someone even younger: Theo Walcott went to the World Cup that summer, despite only being 16 at the time. He didn't see a minute of action, of course, and Eriksson was criticised for effectively wasting a spot in the squad on a work experience kid, but it made perfect sense to me. I would have loved to get that sense of what it was like being at a tournament, the rhythm of it, the dynamic of the squad. Instead, I had to wait for my call-up until Sven had gone and been replaced by Steve McClaren.

Maybe, in hindsight, that was for the best. I had another few months as a Premier League player under my belt, and it meant I didn't feel at all intimidated by being surrounded by all of these stars, by the pressure of representing your country. Others found it harder.

At the time, Joey Barton was the dominant figure at Manchester City. He was the big man. He was the most high-profile player, although it wasn't always for the right reasons. But when he was on it, he was the heart of the team. He was the bite in midfield. He was the one who set the tone. He was a bit like an Asda own-brand Steven Gerrard.

With England, that all changed. He was called up for the first, and only, time in 2007, for a friendly against Spain. It was quite nice, having someone to travel down with, someone you knew from your club in the squad. I was still quite new to it, then, too. Except that the Joey who turned up for England was completely different to the Joey who I knew from City. This new Joey Barton was quiet and nervous, almost shy. At Manchester City, Joey didn't need an invitation to let everyone know what he thought about everything. With England, around the other players, he'd barely say a word. He shrank back into his shell completely. He'd be knocking on my door, asking what time we were meeting, wondering what he needed to bring with him, checking on the schedule for the next day. He'd come and see me and ask what boots we needed for which session, which was a real relief, because it meant that Gerrard hadn't told everyone about what had happened on my first day. Before we went down to dinner, he'd ask where we should sit, and who we should sit with.

That, as it goes, was an important question. It wasn't really a surprise that Joey didn't feel especially comfortable with England when he was called up, because the squad he walked into wasn't the easiest environment to navigate. It wasn't the most welcoming. The players themselves, as people, were fine. Most of them – maybe not *quite* all – were just like Gerrard: they were helpful and humble and friendly. All of those players, all of the golden generation, were so famous that you'd assume they'd be big time, arrogant, up themselves. That was, quite a lot of the time, how they were presented by the media, after all. The reality was totally different. It's amazing, really, quite how wrong the public perception of certain players can be. John Terry, for example: brilliant with young players. You maybe wouldn't expect that, given his status, but he was. Every time someone was called up into the squad for the first time, he'd make a point of greeting them, helping them settle in, having a quiet word with them to make sure they were OK. When I first arrived, he told me that if I ever needed anything, I was to come to him. Rooney, too: you wouldn't imagine, from what you're told about him, that he would be the joker, the live wire, the one who kept the whole camp going. I always felt a little bit sorry for that generation. It's not just that they were built up so much, or that so much was expected of them and they never quite delivered. It's more that they were so famous at the height of that paparazzi era, when footballers became more like mainstream celebrities, but before they had social media which, for all its problems, at least gives people a chance to control their own image. Everyone was obsessed with them. Every mistake they made, on or off the pitch, was highlighted. Fans were led to believe that they knew them in quite a personal way, but it was never the whole picture. The way we think about a lot of them bears no resemblance at all to what they are actually like.

What made England difficult, then, wasn't the players as people. It was how divided the squad was by club loyalty. Looking back, the dynamic was absolutely crazy. There was a large group of Manchester United players: Rio Ferdinand, Wayne Rooney, Paul Scholes, Owen Hargreaves, Wes Brown. That was one faction, and probably the dominant one. Then there was a little Liverpool clan, built around Gerrard and Jamie Carragher. There was a Chelsea gang – Terry, Lampard, Ashley Cole, Joe Cole – and another one from Arsenal. That first evening, when everyone started to arrive at the hotel, could be frosty, especially if we all got together after a big game between two of the big clubs. It would be up to one of the neutrals, someone who wasn't affiliated to any of the major clans, someone like Jermain Defoe, to try to break the ice, to crack a joke about why they all looked so serious, but there was a limit to what any of us could do. I don't think we were ever really united enough as a national team to say that everyone in the squad was talking to everyone else. There was always some sort of beef. It never quite passed over into becoming something you could joke about. It ran deeper than one set of players being disappointed to have lost, or another gloating that they had won. There was a genuine sense that, deep down, they didn't like each other.

That divide defined everything on those England get-togethers. On those trips where we didn't have our own rooms, the Manchester United players would room with each other. Gerrard and Carragher would room together. The Chelsea players would room together, and the Arsenal players. It was the same at mealtimes. There would be a Liverpool table, a United table, a Chelsea table, an Arsenal table, and they were lines that you did not cross. Glen Johnson, who was then at Liverpool, couldn't just wander up and plant himself down next to Rio Ferdinand. That would have been a taboo. It would have been quite helpful, of course, because as a rule your team will probably do better if the players can look each other in the eye, but it was still a taboo. That animosity ran deep.

That left the rest of us, the waifs and strays who had been called up from Manchester City, Everton, Aston Villa, Tottenham and everyone else, on our own table. We were the inbetweeners. That was how I got to know Joleon

Lescott, while he was playing for Everton, and Ashley Young, who first got called up when he was at Watford. I roomed with Joleon on trips. We'd all sit and eat together, trying to have a nice time as the rest of our teammates stared daggers at each other from across the room.

In certain ways, we were an afterthought. The players from the bigger teams did get forms of preferential treatment. Even the post-training massages broke down along club lines. Every evening, every player would expect to get a rub: 10 or 15 minutes lying on a table as a physio worked your muscles, making sure you were ready for the next day. The manager would set aside a time for it to happen: it might have been at 8 p.m., after everyone had finished their dinner.

But then the divide came into play. Manchester United were the most successful team at that point: they had the most trophies, and they had the most players in the England squad. So they would always get the rubs first. Only once all of those players had been up for a massage would the next faction be allowed to go. That might be Chelsea. Then it would be Liverpool. After that, Arsenal. (That's Arsenal's natural position: fourth.) I don't think the order was set in stone, but that was just the way it was; it was almost like an official policy. The rest of us had to wait right until the end for our turn. The masseurs might have been supposed to knock off at 10.30 p.m., but I'd be bowling up at 11, as some bored and weary physio who was just desperate to get to sleep went through the motions on my hamstrings.

And then, as always, things would escalate. After a while, they all decided that they couldn't have just any old physio touching their precious limbs. They had to have someone they knew. From memory, Chelsea were the first to declare that they were bringing their own masseur; they'd summon the person who gave them rubs at club level and instal him with the England squad. The others weren't having that. Soon, Manchester United had their guy, and Liverpool theirs, and so on. It didn't make any difference to the rest of us. We just went to whoever was left, the last masseur standing. I don't think any of us minded, particularly – we didn't know any different – but looking back, it's hard not to feel that this divide is what prevented that England team fulfilling its potential. I can't say for certain, because I never went to a major tournament, but my instinct is that the divide would only have deepened over the course of a whole month in some retreat in South Africa or Poland or Brazil. There was so much tension that they didn't really stand a chance of surviving weeks in each other's company, let alone actually winning something.

There was, after all, definitely enough talent. You could see that in training, especially when you were coming, like me, from a sort of mid-table team. The squad was Champions League standard. Most of them had won it, or would go on to win it; they all played regularly in the quarter- and semi-finals. Then, added to them, you had your young superstars – players like Jack Wilshere, and me – and a clutch of reliable, dependable professionals, good characters and outstanding players like James Milner, Gareth Barry and Joleon. And then, every so often, you'd get someone else called up. Someone who maybe didn't quite fall into any of those groups. Someone who might, in some circumstances, have been known by the rest of the squad as one of the 'shitters'.

I won't name names, of course, because that wouldn't be fair, but England was not an especially comfortable place for them, either. They might have been perfectly good Premier League players. They were obviously perfectly good Premier League players – that's why they'd been called up for England – but they hadn't won a competition or anything. So in that context, against that standard, they just couldn't cope, and everyone knew it.

As always, that first training session would tell the superstars everything they needed to know. The rondo would start, and there'd be one of the new call-ups struggling to match the touch, the skill, the level. And you'd see the mainstays of the squad, their faces slowly changing, their eyes getting wider and their lips pursing in disapproval. They didn't need to say anything. You could see what they were thinking: 'What, exactly, is he doing here?' You'd get confirmation on the bus on the way back from the training ground. 'Did you see him?' someone would ask, in disbelief. 'He was *dreadful*.' There was a bit of allowance made for young players: if you arrived with England at 18 or 19 and struggled in those first few sessions, the rest of the squad understood that you might be nervous, a little too eager to impress, that you might need a bit of time to get used to being around all of these people you'd been watching on TV just a couple of years before. I guess they remembered that it had been just the same for them, when they'd first been called up. The

biggest names in football, the biggest stars of their generation, were always patient and forgiving with young
players. But if you were a bit older, if you were a late
bloomer, if you'd had a good few months for Birmingham
or QPR or someone like that and been called up, if you
were a bit of a surprise inclusion, and you had a stinker,
then that was it. The big dogs would give you a once over
and decide that you didn't belong. You might be the nicest
person in the world. You might be fine for Fulham. But
England isn't for you.

For those of us that stuck around, it changed everything.
There is a financial impact from playing for England,
though it's not a directly lucrative one. Or, at least, it
wasn't once John Terry had decided that he wanted to give
his England fee to charity. The Football Association effectively pays the England players for their time: you'd earn
more if you were called up for longer. So, for an international break that lasted a week, you'd get a cheque – and
at the start, it was an actual cheque – for something like
£10,000 or £20,000. If it was a 10-day get-together, you'd
get a little bit more.

When I was first called up, that was a significant amount
of money. My contract at Manchester City was worth
£5,000 a week then: an England call-up meant picking up
in a few days what it would normally take me a whole
month to make. Or it would have done, if Terry hadn't
decided that it was a bad look to take money for playing
for your country. Instead, he decided that he was going to
donate the bulk of it to good causes. That's obviously
admirable – John Terry is a more complicated character

than people think – and it made perfect sense for him and the rest of the superstars in the squad. They would all have been earning a couple of million a year, at the very least, at that time; they could afford to be as generous as they liked.

It was a bit different for me. I was earning good money, don't get me wrong, but even when you're on £5,000 a week, you notice an extra month's income. You don't lose all proportion. You know that's a lot of money. And while you're happy it's going to a good cause, there is a part of you that wonders if you're being asked to be a little bit more generous than everyone else. You think about asking whether maybe there could be a sliding scale, like you maybe give a proportion of your earnings, rather than a flat rate. But there's no way around it. You can't be the one player who objects. It can't come out that all of the England players are giving their fees to charity, except for Micah, who quite fancies keeping it, thanks very much.

Besides, much more important were the indirect benefits of being an international. Most contracts will contain a clause stating that the player is due a pay hike when they make a certain number of appearances for their country. The one I'd signed when I became a first-team regular at Manchester City certainly did. Once I got to 10 caps, the £5,000-a-week basic salary would jump up to £20,000 a week, to reflect my new status as a recognised international. I was on course to hit that mark at Euro 2008. I was in the team, we would have had a guaranteed three games – maybe more, if the Manchester United and Liverpool players had managed to stay away from each other's throats – and I'd have come back with experience of a major tournament and a pay rise.

Then Scott Carson happened.

Carson was in goal the night in 2007 that we played Croatia at Wembley, the night that Steve McClaren was condemned to be known for the rest of his career as the Wally with the Brolly. Steve is a great coach, and he was very popular with the players; it's a real shame that his time with England ended in such disappointment. He'd made two big decisions that night. He dropped David Beckham, who was playing with LA Galaxy at the time, and he'd chosen Carson ahead of our usual first choice, Paul Robinson. Both of them backfired. Carson was fooled by a shot from Niko Kranjčar early on, and by half-time we were 2–0 down. Beckham came on and almost rescued it – we were level after only a bit more than an hour – but Croatia scored late on. It meant that the golden generation didn't even qualify for the European Championship. It was a national embarrassment. I'd played quite well, but nobody seemed to want to pay any attention to that. I can't quite work out why.

To be fair to Carson, it was a horrible night to be a goalkeeper. It was pouring with rain, and the ground was treacherous. It was the sort of evening when long-range shots that you'd normally easily deal with can become very dangerous indeed. He was devastated after the game, obviously, but I struggled to have too much sympathy with him. If he'd not conceded that early goal, if he'd not been beaten by a routine shot from long distance, I'd have gone to the Euros, and got my 10 caps. That one mistake cost me, over the course of my contract, about £1.5 million. After tax. That still hurts. It cuts me deep. I see Scott quite a lot, now, what with him being Manchester City's third-choice goalkeeper. I run into him quite frequently when I'm back at the Etihad, either for television or in my role as an ambassador. I still find it extremely difficult to look at him and not think that he owes me money.

There was a status thing to playing for England, too. It was, in one way, quite difficult to go back to Manchester City after an international break, like leaving one world and going into another, slightly worse one. You'd have been training with the best players in the country, and then you'd find yourself in a rondo with the Peugeot-driving Javi Garrido. In another way, though, you'd roll into training as a bit of a star. Not just because you played for England, but because of what playing for England gave you access to.

The afternoons on international breaks can be long and, if I'm honest, a bit boring. You do all of your work in the morning. You get up, have breakfast, a quick team meeting to outline the session, do a little gym work to get you nice and warm, go and train, come back, maybe have a bit of a physio session, have lunch. After that, your time is your own until dinner, and then your massage, just before midnight, once Wes Brown has finished. That means, for a few hours every afternoon, there are some very famous, very rich footballers idly sitting around a hotel, searching for something to do. And that acts as a magnet for the kinds of people who make money by selling things to very famous, very rich footballers.

You could buy almost anything on an international break. I don't mean in a shop, though occasionally, the day after a game at Wembley, a few of us might go into London shopping, and then maybe stay out a little later, grab a bite to eat, maybe a couple of drinks, and then, oh, it's late and it's raining, we should probably take shelter in Chinawhite for a little while. No, you could do it all from the comfort of the hotel. There was a jewellery guy who would come to The Grove in the afternoons. There was a watch guy. There was a car company. It could be a very expensive business, playing for England.

I don't know how they came to be allowed in: it may have been that they had a connection to a member of the squad, someone who vouched for them, or possibly to an agent, or maybe even just to someone on staff at the hotel. However it had happened, they were regular features. Everyone bought jewellery from Dave. Players would regularly come back from international duty with a new car: maybe not every time they were called up, but there were some who would definitely upgrade a couple of times a season. You don't need to trawl round dealerships as a player. The dealers come to you, offering you the latest Bentley or R8 or Ferrari, pulling up in the car park to show off whatever the most recent trend would be. Players on the biggest contacts of their lives wouldn't think twice about buying a car off a guy who just turned up at a hotel, not if they trusted them, or if someone they knew trusted them. That was how it was done.

It was on England duty that football felt most like a fantasy to me. It wasn't the real world. It wasn't anywhere

Captain of my Under-9 primary
school team.

Representing Leeds City Boys, 1999.

Celebrating an early Leeds City Boys
cup win with my brother Meshech. I'm
wearing the club tie and jumper!

A team head shot for England
Under-16s.

Playing with the England Under-16s in the Victory Shield match against Scotland in 2003. We drew 1–1 and the two sides shared the trophy as joint winners.

Making my first-team debut for Manchester City at Highbury in October 2005. We lost 1–0, but it was one of the best days of my life.

Heading a last-minute equaliser against Aston Villa in the 5th round of the FA Cup in 2006 – it was my first goal for Manchester City.

Playing in the FA Youth Cup final against Liverpool in 2006.

'Bursting onto the scene' as England's youngest-ever
defender against Holland in November 2006.

Scoring my first international goal in a Euro 2008 qualifier against Israel.

ABOVE: Playing for England in the Euro Under-21 final in 2009, which Germany won 4–0.

LEFT: Celebrating winning the FA Cup in 2011, with Mario Balotelli and Shay Given.

RIGHT: I'll never forget sharing our FA Cup win with the fans in Manchester.

Celebrating with Joe Hart after winning 6-1 at Old Trafford. It felt like we'd made a big statement and taken a giant step towards winning the title.

A career high: winning the league in 2012. It was City's first league title in over 40 years, and I'd had my best season.

It was very special to be chosen to play for Team GB at the Olympics in 2012.

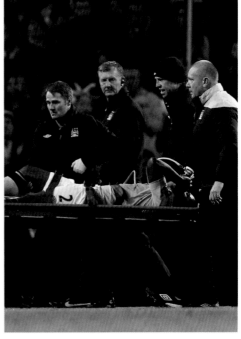

A career low: picking up a serious knee injury early the following season against Swansea. I was out for several months.

TOP (LEFT AND RIGHT): On loan at Fiorentina for the 2014–15 season, where Mohamed 'Mo' Salah became a close teammate and friend. He's one of the nicest, most humble people I've ever met.

RIGHT: Signing a permanent deal to join Aston Villa the following season.

It's an honour to still be involved with City as a club ambassador.

Speaking to my father Lincoln in the *Tackling Racism* documentary in 2021. He has many of my England caps on his table.

LEFT: Debating another *Super Sunday* on Sky with David Jones, Jamie Carragher and Roy Keane.

RIGHT: Being part of the BBC punditry team for the 2021 FA Cup semi-final between Manchester City and Liverpool, with Danny Murphy, Gary Lineker and Alan Shearer.

LEFT: Reminiscing with Roberto Mancini in Florence in January 2022 – we had a lot to catch up on.

close to the real world. You were with people who you had grown up idolising, who seemed to be just ever so slightly better than human – there is something about the way David Beckham dresses that means clothes just look a little nicer on him, almost like they've been designed and cut for his exact body shape – and you suddenly had this vast array of things available just to you.

Obviously, when you went back to your club, that made you a bit of a trend-setter. You were their window into what the elite were doing: what the latest watch was, or what the new must-have car might be, or what you could put a load of diamonds on now. I would go back to Manchester City with my chest puffed out even more than it normally was. Inside the camp, you might have been an inbetweener. You might have had to wait for a massage, and sit at the outcasts table when you had dinner, but outside it, none of that mattered. All that counted was that you were an England player. You were one of the chosen ones, one of the elite. You had arrived.

9

A BOTTOMLESS LIST OF PLAYERS WHO SHOULD REPLACE ME

The first we heard of it, in the dressing room, was after it had happened. That's not all that unusual. Players are often the last to know what's going on at their own club. Most of the time, that's absolutely fine. We take care of our own business. We turn up, we train, we play, we go home. There's no point worrying about the things you can't control.

We hadn't been warned that Manchester City was about to be sold. We didn't know there was a takeover coming, or that one of the richest people on the planet – a man who was in charge of a whole country – was about to transform the team. We just woke up one morning and the club we knew had changed beyond recognition. We had money. We had power. We had ambition. The sky was the limit. Manchester City were going to be a superpower, and it would all be down to Thaksin Shinawatra, the prime minister of Thailand and our new boss.

Among the players, there were two reactions to the news. Half of the lads were rubbing their hands with glee.

They were wheeling around the training ground, hand in the air like Alan Shearer, as though they'd just scored a last-minute winner. The average wage at City, at the time, must have been about £20,000 a week. A rich new owner would mean that increased. Substantially. For those of us who were established in the team, who felt our places were secure, this was good news. The other half of the squad, the ones who thought they might be vulnerable, were the opposite. They were devastated. They knew that if the club started going places, it would be without them. They'd be replaced at the first available opportunity.

In the end, of course, neither of those things happened. I'd be lying if I said Thaksin wasn't good for me. He gave the green light to the five-and-a-half-year contract I signed at City, the longest deal in the club's history. But whether he was good for the club is a different matter. His owner-ship style was a bit unusual, put it that way. Every international break, he'd take a selection of players off to Thailand for some commercial deal. No harm in that – I'd been to Thailand before, and there are far worse places to spend a few days – but it doesn't exactly suggest that your priorities are the football.

Then, of course, there was the political situation. There's always one busy player in a dressing room. A gossiper. A rumour-monger. A party-pooper. Someone who missed their calling and ended up being a footballer when they should really have been a rolling 24-hour news channel. 'Have you heard that they're freezing his assets?' they'd come in and say. 'He's going to be forced to sell.' 'There's going to be a coup.' To most of us, it was too distant to be meaningful. We didn't have a grasp on Thai politics. The only follow-up question any of us ever had was simple. 'Are we going to get paid at the end of the month?' There's no point worrying about the things you can't control.

As far as I know, we did get paid at the end of the month, no matter how desperate Thaksin's situation grew. But the party-pooper had been right. He was not going to be at City for long. He lasted just a year, in fact, and then we had another morning where we discovered that the club we knew had changed beyond recognition. Again, nobody had mentioned anything to the players. Again, we were getting our updates from the yellow ticker on Sky Sports News. Again, our dressing-room busybody went into overdrive. 'We're proper now,' he told us. 'This time it's a whole country.'

The way we reacted can probably be traced to what had happened with Thaksin. His arrival hadn't suddenly made City successful. He hadn't been able to attract a load of the best players in the world to Eastlands. We were still Manchester City. We still had three technical players, a strike force of Rolando Bianchi and Bernardo Corradi, and a team full of square pegs in round holes. Even when we googled them, even when we saw just how much money they had, we were probably a little sceptical. Another takeover? Abu Dhabi this time, is it? Who's next?

You could see straightaway that the new owners were different. Early on, Khaldoon al-Mubarak, the chairman, invited me for a chat. I'd only just turned 20, but I was a senior player by then. He wanted to outline their plan for the club. In the space of ten years, they wanted not just to win the Premier League, the FA Cup and the Champions League, but redevelop Manchester, bringing jobs and homes. It's a Gary Neville phrase, now, but they wanted us to be 'best in class' at everything. It sounded great. Very impressive. Music to my ears. Khaldoon was a serious, charismatic person. But I knew things were easier said than done. Thaksin had taught us that. Besides, I thought, which world-class players would really come to Manchester City? You had Manchester United right next door. Chelsea had just made the Champions League final. Liverpool and Arsenal still had all the prestige they'd built up over decades. Who would want to sign for us?

The answer, it turned out, was Robinho. Within a few hours of the takeover being announced, the owners had made him the first signing of the new era. It was jaw-dropping. An incredible coup. The sort of thing that Thaksin had never been able to do. Manchester City – the team that until recently had Antoine Sibierski up front – had just signed a Brazil forward from Real Madrid who had once been declared the twenty-first-century version of Pelé.

It's easy to overlook how important Robinho was to Manchester City. Not so much on the pitch, admittedly, though that wasn't entirely his fault. He had talent to burn. He wasn't especially quick or strong, but you could see from the first moment that he had quality. He could do things other players wouldn't even be able to imagine. He went past players as though they weren't there. He had this one drop of the shoulder that seemed to happen almost in slow motion, but there was absolutely nothing you could do to stop it. He was a level above everyone else at City at the time. I have no idea what he must have thought when he had his first training session. He'd been at Real Madrid. He'd played alongside Raúl and Guti and David Beckham and Zinedine Zidane. Now he had Gelson Fernandes in midfield.

If anything, that was the problem. The season after he arrived, our game plan basically became: 'Get the ball to Robinho.' His reputation and his price-tag meant that the fans and the media expected him to score a hat-trick in every game. He was this big Brazilian superstar, one of the best players in the world, and it was almost a challenge to him: go on then, if you're so good, let's see you do it in the Premier League. The issue was that the players were so in awe of him that they almost took the same approach. We thought he'd be able to win games single-handedly, so that was kind of what we asked him to do. It meant he was always destined to be a bit of a disappointment. He didn't speak much English, but he had a little core of Brazilians around him – we already had Elano and Jô at the club – and he was a smiling, personable presence in the dressing room. He was always dancing. I helped him find a couple of barbers in Manchester. I don't know how I did that, other than by miming scissors and then handing him a phone number, but it helped us bond. But no matter how well he settled, it didn't matter. He was too good for us, at that stage. We weren't ready for him. Not yet, anyway.

His real impact was off the pitch. Signing Robinho made everybody sit up and take notice of what was happening at City. It was a message to the rest of football from the owners: we're here, and we're serious. He changed the way other players thought of City, too. He was supposed to sign for Chelsea, a team who had just made the Champions League final, only for that deal to fall apart because Real Madrid pulled the plug when Chelsea announced it a little too early on their website. I think they'd even started selling shirts with his name on them. That gave City an opening, and they swooped. Let's be honest: they didn't convince him to come by telling him about their ten-year plan and trying to sell him on the idea of a project. They convinced him to come by offering him a massive salary. But whatever the reason, his arrival made it acceptable for other players of that level to think of City as a viable option. Players are like sheep. They follow what others have done. Nobody wants to be first. Nobody wants to take a risk. Nobody wants to be an outlier. Robinho removed all of those worries. The ambition of the owners meant that City would have been able to attract the best players eventually. But Robinho made it all happen a lot quicker.

His arrival turned football upside down. It would have been even more spectacular had the other deal the club was working on that day come off: they were trying to snatch Dimitar Berbatov, the Spurs striker, from under the noses of Manchester United. That would have been even more of a statement of intent. As it was, Robinho was enough. City's fans went mad. Out of nowhere, the club they'd supported all their lives, one that had a reputation as a lovable underdog, one that had always existed in United's shadow, one that had made them suffer in a million different strange and hilarious ways, was capable of signing someone from Real Madrid. It wasn't exactly a well-trodden path. Steve McManaman might have done it, but I can't imagine Alfredo Di Stéfano had ever been offered the chance to move to Maine Road, or Madrid had come knocking for Steve Redmond.

The press was just as breathless. All of a sudden the papers were full of stories talking about how City were now the richest club in the world. The assumption was that Robinho would be the first of many. Soon, there would be a whole parade of *galácticos* on show at Eastlands. It wasn't just excitement. It was a frenzy.

The only people who didn't really share it were the players. We all knew it was brilliant for the club, obviously. And we all – or most of us, anyway – wanted the club to be successful. It matters to you. As a player, you develop a bond to pretty much every club you play for. Coming through at City means that my love for them is stronger than it is for any of the other teams I joined, but I still have a soft spot for Aston Villa and Fiorentina. I want them both to do well. Just not as well as City.

But that isn't your only motivation. Your own ambitions, your own job security, your own role matter to you as well. You want the team to succeed, but ideally you want the team to succeed with you in it. In those first few weeks after the takeover, that was what every player in the dressing room was asking themselves. What does this mean for me?

I think we struggled with it, to be honest. A dressing room can't be united when nobody really knows what the future looks like for them. I was relatively confident that I would survive whatever was coming: I was young, I was playing for England, I didn't feel like I was the weak link in the squad. You very rarely heard anyone say that the real problem with Manchester City was the international right-back. But the sudden change in the club's outlook created a divide in the dressing room. Some players backed their ability. They decided they would rise to the challenge. It went down less well with some of the others. They started to look over their shoulders, try to work out an exit strategy. That starts to affect your focus. You can't commit yourself fully to a team if you're worried about where you might have to go next. Everything started to become very tense.

That got worse as the months wore on and the first full transfer window under the new owners, January 2009, came into view. It felt to most of us as though we were doing OK. Results weren't too bad. We were performing well enough. But in those days we would have newspapers in the canteen or in the dressing room, and it started to feel like the club was just waiting for the right moment to replace every single one of us. A different name would be linked with a move to us almost every single day. You couldn't really avoid it. You might learn not to pick up the papers, not to check the internet, not to seek it out deliberately, but you'd still hear about it. Your mates might text you, asking if it was true that soon you'd be playing alongside Zlatan Ibrahimović or whoever. Or your agent would call, checking in, wondering if you wanted him to go and ask the club what the plans were for you individually. It was hard not to be distracted by it.

That's not to say that some of the developments weren't exciting. That January, the club made a big push to sign Kaká from AC Milan. He'd just won the Ballon d'Or, and in the days before Lionel Messi and Cristiano Ronaldo left everyone else in the dust, he was regarded as probably the best player on the planet. I would genuinely have loved us to sign Kaká, slotting him in as a number 10 with Robinho out wide. That would have been a bit of an upgrade from playing for a team where the man you turned to, if you really needed a goal in a crucial game, was David James, your goalkeeper.

But then it was easy for me to be excited by the idea of Kaká, because he didn't play in my position. Nobody was suggesting they bring in a Brazilian playmaker and put him at right-back. It was much worse when you were the one threatened by the supposed big new signing.

The worst were the 'dream teams'. The papers had decided that Manchester City were going to build the first billion-pound team, an all-star XI of the best players on the planet. Someone would publish one almost every day, including whichever player was apparently now a target for the club. There'd be Wayne Rooney up front with David Villa, and Cristiano Ronaldo out wide, and a defence built around John Terry. At most, they'd leave one or two of the current team in. For a while, I was one of the lucky ones. There'd be all these big stars and then me, Micah Richards, the man they couldn't upgrade.

And then it was my turn. The first right-back City were linked with was Dani Alves. I'd be lying if I said I was happy about it, but fair enough: Alves was probably the best right-back in the world, a key part of the all-conquering team Pep Guardiola was building at Barcelona. If you're going to be dropped for anyone, it might as well be Dani Alves. Then, a couple of weeks later, it would be another Brazilian, Maicon. Again, it would be a bit arrogant to complain too much. Maicon was probably the second-best right-back in the world, at least until he got destroyed by Gareth Bale in a Champions League game at the San Siro. Still, that can happen to anyone. Bale was by a long way the toughest opponent I ever faced. Not just because he was rapid, and strong, and had a shot that should have been governed by some sort of arms treaty, but because he never stopped. You'd get to 70 minutes or so and think you'd done OK, you'd kept him quiet. But even as you started to slow down, as all that effort started to tell, he'd still be charging at you, full speed, fresh as a daisy. Anyone could get destroyed by Gareth Bale. It's no great shame it happened to Maicon.

It was when the targets started to get a little less glamorous that I took a bit of offence. It's one thing being told by the newspapers that you're being replaced by one of the best players of all time in your position, and quite another to flick through the sports pages to find out that your club is planning to dump you in favour of Glen Johnson. I've got nothing against Glen Johnson. He was a good player. Technically, he was excellent. He had a great left foot, too, which meant he was dangerous cutting inside. He scored quite a few goals, for a full-back. But he wasn't as explosive as me. He wasn't as quick, or as strong, or as dynamic. You've got all the money and ambition in the world and you've decided that what you really have to do is replace me with Glen Johnson?

In reality, of course, the change was a lot more gradual. The first summer, most of the new arrivals came from other teams in the Premier League: Gareth Barry, Emmanuel Adebayor, Kolo Touré and Carlos Tevez. I played a bit of a role in one of them. I'd got to know Joleon Lescott with England – we roomed together – and Mark Hughes, City's manager, asked me if I might sound him out to see if he'd be interested in leaving Everton to come to Manchester. I did my job. I mentioned it to Joleon, and he said he'd leap at the chance. He went on to win the Premier League a couple of times, medals that I think deep down he knows he owes to me. What I found out later was that I'd only been given half the story. City did want to sign Joleon. But they wanted to sign him to take my place: they'd been working on a deal to sell me to Everton at exactly the same time as I was pitching Joleon on the idea of coming to Manchester.

It wasn't until Roberto Mancini arrived that the big stars started to come in. David Silva, Yaya Touré and Mario Balotelli all signed in the space of a few weeks in 2010, as well as the likes of Edin Džeko, James Milner and Aleksandar Kolarov. It was the shake-up the squad needed. A lot of the players who had been at City before the new owners came in had been given improved contracts. A few egos had grown in line with their wages. After those difficult few months immediately after the takeover, when everything seemed so uncertain and nobody really knew what was going on, maybe the squad was now too comfortable. Mancini was having none of it. He made it clear that he had the whole market at his mercy. He could basically sign who he wanted. You either gave him everything, or he'd sell you in a heartbeat.

Fortunately, I landed on the right side of that line. Mancini liked how hard I worked, enough to tell Balotelli that he could learn a lot from me. He wanted Mario to have my attitude, and in exchange I needed to learn how to score goals like him. That was the deal, as Mancini saw it. That seemed a bit unfair, given that he was a striker and I wasn't, but I took the compliment.

There were a few of us who survived all that change, all that uncertainty. In the space of two years, almost everyone else had gone: not just the players who had been at City before the new owners, but some of those who had come in early on. Even Robinho, the player who started everything, had departed, returning to Brazil on loan. The team had gone from not being good enough for a player of that quality to being so good that he wasn't really playing. Only half a dozen of us or so were left. Joe Hart was still our goalkeeper. Vincent Kompany was still the captain. Me and Pablo Zabaleta were still competing for the right-back spot. Shaun Wright-Phillips, who came back just before the takeover, was still around. And so, most impressively of all, was Jô, a Brazilian striker we had signed a month or so before Robinho arrived and had gone on to score an incredible four goals for the club. For all of us, it would prove worth it.

As a kid, it had never occurred to me that I might win the Premier League one day. Even once I joined City, it wasn't the sort of thing we thought about. Manchester City didn't win Premier League titles. That was the sort of thing that Manchester United and Chelsea did. It would have been enough for me to play in the Premier League. That was as far as my ambition went.

The FA Cup was different. That felt realistic, somehow. Not just because you knew that sometimes an underdog might win it – Wimbledon or Portsmouth – or, like Newcastle or Aston Villa or Everton, make the final, or because you could always hope for a kind route to Wembley, but because we had a bit of experience with cup runs. In 2006, City had gone all the way to the final of the FA Youth Cup. We'd had an incredible team: so good, in fact, that I didn't even start one of the games. Michael Johnson was in that side, in midfield with Kelvin Etuhu. Daniel Sturridge was up front. Youth football can be weird. Few of the Liverpool team we played in the final went on to have stellar careers: the likes of Stephen Darby, Jay Spearing and Jack Hobbs were solid pros rather than superstars. In the Youth Cup, it turned out that we had all the star names. We still lost. It showed us, though, that we could get to a cup final. More than anything, the FA Cup had always felt like the trophy I could win.

We would do so in Mancini's first full season. I've never been as nervous as I was before that FA Cup final. We were overwhelming favourites, heavily fancied to beat Stoke City, and normally I never had trouble sleeping before a game, even a big one. Manchester derbies, Bayern Munich in the Champions League, all of it: I slept like a log. I don't really get anxious. I was always pretty relaxed.

I never felt the pressure. If anything, it always felt like I raised my game on big occasions, just so long as Franck Ribéry wasn't involved.

But the tension around that final was too much even for me. I tossed and turned all night. I woke up again and again, drenched in sweat. I'd been at City for almost ten years. I knew full well how long the club had been waiting for a trophy: 35 years, and even longer for the cup itself. It was something I'd grown up with, something I'd bought into. I was desperate to win something for myself, of course, but more than anything I was desperate to win something for City.

As it turned out, I didn't need to worry. Yaya Touré hadn't had any trouble sleeping, and neither had Mario Balotelli. Yaya scored the goal that won the game, and Mario put in one of his best performances during his time in England. We were far too good for Stoke. I had my trophy, and City had theirs.

In hindsight, though, the most significant game in that run might not have been the final. It might have been the semi. That was the other thing you learned at City's academy: that nothing is quite as sweet as beating Manchester United. That's why all of those derbies, before the trophies started to flow and the balance of power in the city changed, were always seen as such crucial occasions. United were our ultimate test. We knew we had to prove we were better than them to achieve everything we wanted.

The way players feel about this sort of rivalry isn't quite the same as the fans. I wasn't from Manchester. I hadn't grown up with it, though as someone from Leeds who supported Arsenal, it's probably fair to say that even as a kid I wasn't especially fond of United. That changed into something deeper the longer I spent at City. There was always an arrogance to the United players, even at youth level. You always got the sense that they thought they were better than you, just because they were wearing red, and you were wearing blue. Playing for United meant more than playing for City.

It was the same with the first team. They had a swagger. They acted like they owned the town. You'd see them out, in a bar or a club, and they'd be acting the big dogs. Don't get me wrong: they'd earned that. They'd won however many titles. They'd been champions of Europe. They'd done it all. They were one of the best teams England has ever seen. But that doesn't mean you have to enjoy it when they're rubbing it in your face. It was what made the rare occasions when we beat them, early on, even more special. You felt like you were taking out years of frustration on them, putting them back in their box.

Beating them at Wembley in the semi-final, ending their hopes of doing another treble – they ended up with just the title that year, because they went back to Wembley for the Champions League final and got taken apart by Barcelona – wasn't just satisfying, it felt like a watershed. It was a psychological barrier that we'd overcome. We'd been up against United in a big game, a winner-takes-all sort of a match, and we'd come out on top. That wasn't what usually happened. It wasn't what had happened for years. But it had happened now, and that was important.

If there was any doubt of that, it disappeared about seven months later, when we went to Old Trafford and won 6–1. Our preparations for the game hadn't been perfect – thanks to Samir Nasri and his temper – but it didn't matter in the slightest. This was the day that whatever inferiority complex we might have had about them disappeared. Winning at Old Trafford felt good. Winning by five goals at Old Trafford felt better. The best thing, though, was seeing that we had absolutely nothing to fear from them. It was the first time we knew, for certain, that our squad was just as good as theirs. Better, in fact. I'd been in teams that had beaten them before, but they'd always been underdog victories. We'd had to dig in. We'd had to fight. We'd had to make sure they didn't get the chance to play. Our win at Old Trafford was the first time I'd ever looked at United and known we had nothing to fear.

It was exactly what we needed. We never really talked, as a squad, about whether we could win the title the following year. We didn't sit down at the start of the season and say that was our objective. It would come up occasionally, normally when Mancini told us we didn't have a hope of managing it if we didn't stop being 'shit without Yaya'. We expected to be in contention for it, of course. We wanted to get to April or May and have a shot at it. But United were still favourites. They were the reigning champions. They'd been to two of the last three Champions League finals. Sir Alex Ferguson knew how to win, and how to keep winning. Our aim was to keep pace with them for as long as we could.

The 6–1 showed us that we could aim a little higher. But still, nobody wanted to talk about it. Players are superstitious. There was no rule, no ban on talking about it – bans were reserved for important things, things that made a difference, like making sure nobody wore anything purple – but it was something we all silently agreed on. It was almost like mentioning it might jinx it.

That held all the way through the season, right up until the final game. We knew, the night before we played QPR, that all we had to do was win, and City's first title in 44 years would be ours. The first phase of the ten-year plan that Khaldoon had laid out to us all that first day would be over, on time and on what was basically an unlimited budget. Mission accomplished. We didn't want to tempt fate, though. When one player pointed out at dinner that it was just one more game, one more win, and that was it, we would be champions, he was shouted down immediately. Things were still finely balanced. We were level on points with Manchester United, and only ahead of them on goal difference. It was enough of a lead – eight goals – to know they'd have to do something really unlikely to overhaul us if we won our game, but still: the slightest slip could be costly. We had no margin for error.

Roughly an hour into the game the next day, the player who had decided to break the code of silence would have been getting plenty of dirty looks. Manchester United were winning at Sunderland, and we were losing at home to a team that was battling relegation. We'd taken the lead, through Pablo Zabaleta, but then conceded twice after the break. At the Stadium of Light, they were busy preparing the trophy presentation for United. At the Etihad, the fans were starting to lose hope. You could hear them groaning and grumbling. 'Typical City,' they kept saying. It was, too. This is what City did: they found a way to get as close as possible to success, and then threw it all away at the last. It had all the ingredients. QPR needed to win to be sure of staying up. They had three former City players – Joey Barton, Shaun Wright-Phillips and Nedum Onuoha – on the pitch, and a former City manager on the bench. Mark Hughes had been sacked to make way for Roberto Mancini. It's probably fair to assume he would have enjoyed denying his successor the Premier League title, and sending it to his mentor, Alex Ferguson, instead. It couldn't have been more typically City.

I could hear all of those complaints first-hand, because I spent the game as a substitute. I'd been the starting right-back for most of that season. I'd played the majority of games in the Premier League, but then I pulled my hamstring at the end of March. I was only ruled out for a couple of weeks, but Mancini's rule was always that he didn't change the team if we were doing well. Pablo had replaced me, and that was that; until he made a mistake, or we lost a game, he was first choice.

Two competing thoughts run through your mind at a time like that. Of course you want the team to win. Of course you want to win the title. You've contributed enough. You'll deserve your medal. It's different, as I would find out later, if you've been nothing but a bit-part player. When we won the league in 2014, I'd barely been on the pitch. I'd only played 10 games all season, and only two of them were in the Premier League. Once we'd won the title, I was sent out on to the pitch with the rest of the squad, but I knew I hadn't actually qualified for a medal; back then, you needed to have made a certain number of appearances to get one. It was humiliating. I felt like an impostor, not just like I'd invited myself to someone else's party, but like I was now pretending I'd planned it and done the drinks and the food.

But in 2012, I knew I'd played my part. I could tell myself that I'd helped, even if I had to watch the final few games from the bench. That's easier said than done. In those last few weeks, all I wanted to do was play. That QPR game was the worst. Even before it started, I knew it would probably be the biggest game of my career. It would be the game when Manchester City finally won the title, after all those years, when the banner keeping track of the club's wait for a championship that had hung at Old Trafford for so long finally had to come down. And I wouldn't be playing in it.

Still, I had a bit of hope. As a rule, Mancini would wait until we had taken the lead and then, around about an hour in, he'd send a defender on to shore things up. You know what they say: you can take the manager out of Italy, but you can't take the Italy out of a manager who's sitting on a slender lead. In normal circumstances, I'd have come on for the last 20 or 30 minutes, just enough to see the game out. That would have been fine for me.

That game, though, was just about as far from normal circumstances as you can imagine. We did take the lead, but it was Zabaleta who scored it. Zabaleta never scored.

It was his first goal of the season. It was only the fourth goal he'd ever scored in the Premier League. He was roughly as prolific as Jô. That made it much less likely that he'd come off. And then, as QPR equalised and then took the lead, it became impossible. We didn't need to shore things up now. We needed to score two goals, or all the work that we'd put in that season – and all the work the owners had put in over the last four years – would go up in smoke. Mancini wasn't about to start throwing on defenders.

I'd started that day feeling a bit sorry for myself. I wanted to play. I wanted to be out there. It's not exactly admirable, not especially team-spirited, but that's how players think. It's how they have to think. You wouldn't ever want your team to lose just because you're a substitute, but put it this way: I was probably hoping Zabaleta had a stinker, or had to come off for some reason. Not an injury – I'd never wish an injury on another player – but maybe his head went. Maybe he got an early booking. Maybe he suddenly developed a really heavy cold. The thought of losing the title at the very last concentrated my mind, though. I was devastated not to be playing, but from that point on, all that mattered was City scoring twice, and winning the league. I'd rather get a champion's medal for not playing than not get a champion's medal at all.

As time wore on, though, I was getting more and more nervous. The goal wouldn't come. The fans were muttering. 'We're going to blow it.' 'We always blow it.' 'Typical City.' I felt powerless. It was Balotelli who picked me up.

We'd been sent out to warm up – I have no idea why I was there, I wasn't coming on – and, just like any fan, we were kicking every ball. Mario could clearly tell that I was suffering. He will have known how much it meant to me, because it meant just as much to him. 'Don't worry,' he said. 'We'll win this.' He sounded completely confident. And he was, because Mario was always confident in himself. 'I'll come on, and I'll score or assist.' He promised me he'd win us the game.

That's what makes a big player, I think. They have that self-belief. If it's strong enough, it's almost like it makes things happen. Balotelli did go on. He was on the pitch when Edin Džeko, two minutes into injury time, drew us level. You could feel the stadium change. We still needed another goal. We only had a couple of minutes. United had finished by then; they thought they'd won the title. But for the first time since QPR had gone ahead, I believed that we could do it.

It was at that point that Mario intervened. He hadn't created a single goal that season. It was his only assist in the Premier League in his entire career at Manchester City. But he found a pass to pick out Sergio Agüero in the box, with four minutes of injury time already gone. It was the last kick of the game, and the last kick of the season. It was like something out of a children's story book. And only Sergio could have scored it; only Sergio would have had the presence of mind to take the extra touch that created the angle; only Sergio would have been relaxed enough, calm enough, not to swipe at the ball at the first opportunity. You need big players for big moments. And that was probably the biggest moment of all. There will never be another title win like that, even if İlkay Gündoğan and City did their best to emulate it in 2022. Everything that happened after that is a bit of a blur. I ran down the touchline with the rest of the squad to meet Sergio, I think. Roberto Mancini celebrated by telling the world to fuck off. He was never happier than when telling people to fuck off. There was a pitch invasion. There was a presentation. There was a party. And at the end of it, I had a medal round my neck.

Some of the players on the pitch that day were always going to win trophies. Yaya, Balotelli, Tevez, Agüero: wherever they had ended up, they would have been champions. But there is something extra special in doing it as an academy player. The Manchester City I joined never dreamed of becoming Premier League champions. That wasn't even on our radar. And now we'd done it. We'd beaten Chelsea and we'd beaten Liverpool and we'd even beaten the Manchester United of Alex Ferguson. That last one mattered. We'd beaten all of those great teams, and the greatest manager of all time. The plan had come together, at last.

10

FRANK LAMPARD IS INSIDE MY HEAD

Frank Lampard didn't say anything. I was standing in the tunnel at Stamford Bridge, waiting to go out on the pitch, and he walked straight past me. He didn't acknowledge me at all. No subtle nod of the head, no look of recognition. Nothing. It was only a week or so earlier that I'd been training alongside him for England. We hadn't become best mates or anything: Frank was one of the quieter players in the squad, almost shy, and our paths hadn't really crossed.

But still, I'd always assumed that once you were an England player, once you had that status, then on some level you were teammates. There's a bit of a code of honour among fellow internationals. You might have a bit of a giggle with each other in the tunnel. You might even have a chat out on the pitch. You see it all time, Paul Pogba and N'Golo Kanté grabbing a quick word, covering their mouths so that – you imagine – nobody can see Pogba complaining about how all of his teammates at club level are worse than the ones he has with France. Once the game starts, you go in just as hard as you would with anybody else, but there's never any afters. You don't want any bad blood carrying over into the next squad, after all. There's a respect.

That was how both the Coles, Joe and Ashley, had approached it. They'd been in the England squad with me, too; that afternoon, even though they were playing for Chelsea and I had a Manchester City shirt on, they made a point of saying hello. Only Lampard seemed to ignore me. Looking back, it's probably fair to say I didn't handle it especially well. You might even say I was just the tiniest bit childish about it.

Chelsea against Manchester City was not quite as big, then, as it is now. This was 2007, a year before the take-over, and our team sheet that day proved it. This was Sven-Göran Eriksson's Manchester City. Javi Garrido was the left-back. Giorgios Samaras led the line. Dietmar Hamann, who was then in his mid-thirties, marshalled our midfield. With a team like that, it might be a bit of a surprise to learn that we'd made quite a good start to the season. We'd won four games in a row. A couple of months in, we looked like we might even be able to push for Europe. Chelsea, meanwhile, were in a bit of a mess. They'd sacked José Mourinho for the first time a few weeks before, and though they'd not lost since, nobody thought very much of their caretaker manager, Avram Grant. People were still talking about them as a crisis club.

As we walked out of the tunnel, lined up to shake hands and trotted off to our positions, though, I wasn't thinking about any of that. I wasn't even thinking about what Sven had told us before the game, or how he'd asked us to play. All I could think about was the fact that Frank Lampard hadn't said hello to me. 'Who does he think he is? We were only together last week. We're both England players, but now he thinks he's better than me?' I can't be sure that I wasn't saying all of that out loud. The only thing on my mind, from that point on, was making sure Frank Lampard knew exactly who I was. I was going to smash him, and I was going to smash him early.

To my credit, that's exactly what I did. The first chance I had, I went straight through him. There was a little bit of a flare-up afterwards: maybe Frank didn't think the code of honour applied, seeing as he seemed to have no memory of meeting me whatsoever. I felt good. I felt like I'd made a point. I felt like he'd think twice about ignoring me again. Sadly, that was about as good as my afternoon got. There wasn't much credit for me after that. The remaining 89 minutes, plus injury time, count as what is probably the single worst game of football I've ever played. A game so bad that from the outside you'd be forgiven for wondering whether I'd ever played football before.

Let's walk through my mistakes for the goals. For the first, Lampard slipped a ball into a channel for Michael Essien. For some reason, I walked the other way, like I had noticed something really interesting on the other side of the penalty area. Essien scored. For the second, Lampard curled a ball with the outside of his boot into the path of Didier Drogba. It was, in all fairness, a really good ball. I could have cut it out, though, if I had not momentarily forgotten which foot went in front of the other. Drogba scored. Salomon Kalou walked past me for the third. He didn't need to do much else, because on the highlights it would appear that I have just stopped moving. For the fourth, I was left in the dust by Joe Cole, who has not gone down in history as one of the fastest players to grace the Premier League. For the fifth, I dropped back and then, inexplicably, stepped forward, a movement that succeeded in both playing Kalou onside and giving him about ten minutes to think about where he wanted to put the ball. Andriy Shevchenko scored the sixth. I remember being incredibly excited when Chelsea signed Shevchenko from AC Milan. He'd been one of the best strikers in Europe for years. Not many true superstars came to the Premier League, back then, but Shevchenko was every inch a superstar. It didn't take long to see why Milan had been willing to sell him. He was on the decline. His movement was just as good as it had always been, but he'd lost just a little bit of a pace. He had a tricky time in England, and he went down as a bit of a flop. But he looked like his old self that day. That's how badly I played.

Watching those goals back, I'm not entirely sure what I'm doing. My head had gone completely. I couldn't do basic things. I couldn't remember when to hold the line and when to step out. I could barely remember how to run. At least one of the goals makes it look like I'd even forgotten how to fall over to block a ball, and if you can't even fall over, then you're really in trouble. All of the goals had been my fault, but the ones that came direct from Lampard somehow felt even worse. And it had all happened because someone I didn't know especially well hadn't said hello to me, and I'd decided to be mortally offended.

All defeats hurt. Even a run-of-the-mill loss in an average Premier League game can take a few days to work itself out of your system. Losing bigger games – a derby, or a title showdown, or a Champions League game – can stay with you for weeks. Every so often, there'll be a story about players going out for a meal or to a bar after a significant defeat, as though it's outrageous that they're out enjoying themselves when they should be at home, hiding under a duvet and licking their wounds.

That reaction is the wrong way round. Being a footballer is a privileged life, obviously. It is not just the money, and the fame, and the lifestyle that all of that brings. It's the fact that you can do the thing you dreamed about, the thing that millions of people dreamed about, for a living.

It might be incredibly difficult to get there, but once you do, you're one of the privileged few: you might be released, you might have to fight back, you will almost certainly have to make sacrifices and deal with setbacks. But once you're in, it looks like a pretty easy life. And it looks like a pretty easy life because, in a lot of ways, it is. You're pampered. You're looked after. You don't have to worry about anything. You don't have to acquire basic life skills. There's a reason that a lot of players struggle to adapt once they've retired. During your career, everything is done for you. If your washing machine goes, you call someone at your club, and they send someone out to fix it. You don't have to know a plumber. You don't have to book your own travel. You don't have to pack your own bags. If my mum hadn't made me do the hoovering or the washing-up when I was a kid, I could easily have got to the end of my career and had no idea how to look after myself. Football wants players to think about nothing but football.

There's a security, too. You know that no matter how much your form goes, there's a decent chance that someone will come in and sign you anyway and pay you tens of thousands of pounds a week to play badly for them. There's a decent chance it will be Sunderland or QPR, or at least there was when I was playing. You're protected from all of the things that most people have to worry about almost every day.

But there is a flip side. You know that any defeat affects hundreds of thousands, millions of people. Your bad day at work is beamed out live to a global television audience. Everything you do is pored over and picked at, and every single thing you and your teammates do wrong is analysed by people up and down the country. That creates a ridiculous amount of pressure. The fact players might go out after a defeat isn't a sign that they don't care. It's the opposite. It's their attempt to try and deal with it.

It's not easy to have sympathy for footballers, and most footballers don't expect any. They know that elite players are paid more money than anyone could ever possibly need simply to do a couple of hours' work a day. It's not quite right to say that they're lucky – far too much hard work goes into it to say that any player is 'lucky' to have a career – but they know how fortunate they are. They know that they get all of that money because of the pressure. It's in the terms and conditions of the job. But that doesn't mean they know how to handle it.

You saw it with previous generations. There is a reason why, for a long time, English football had such a strong drinking culture. It was how the players of the 1960s, 70s and 80s coped with their disappointments, with the pressure. They didn't have access to any sort of psychological support. There was nobody they could go and talk to about their fears or their anxieties or the difficulties they were facing. They couldn't even talk to their teammates or their coaches about it. The culture within football has always been that you do not show any weakness. No matter what you're going through, what you're struggling with, whether it's at work or at home, you don't admit to it. You swallow it down. You deal with it. You take it on the chin. Even when I was playing, which is not as long ago as it might seem, you would be told to 'man up'. Admitting you found something difficult was seen, by other players facing exactly the same issues, not as a sign that you needed to be supported. It would be seen as proof that you weren't strong enough, that you didn't have the right mentality. A club wouldn't offer to get you help. They'd be more likely to sell you, to make you someone else's problem.

That has started to change in the last few years. I don't think it is perfect now, by any means, and I'm pretty sure that the last place anyone dealing with something incredibly difficult would want to be is a football dressing room, but most teams will offer their players access to a psychologist. There is much more awareness of mental health issues.

Players are seen less as machines and more as human beings. Managers are much more understanding. Clubs are much more concerned with the culture they create.

But players still need a way to find that release, to cope with disappointment. They have to find ways of drowning their sorrows. Many still drink, of course, but sports science means it's probably not sinking a dozen pints: it might be champagne or vodka, something that isn't quite so bloating. Others will gamble, or buy cars, or watches, or whatever might be in fashion at the time. It's not exactly surprising that quite a lot of young men try to find a bit of a solace in meeting women. And it's not a shock that, after a defeat, sometimes they want to go out. They want the release. Whatever they do, whatever their vice, it is a coping mechanism. They're trying to make themselves feel better.

Strangely, that can be true after success, too. Nobody gets criticised for celebrating a big win, obviously, or for having a party after lifting a trophy. Nobody objects when Jack Grealish is quite clearly just a little bit the worse for wear on Manchester City's victory parade. But winning something leaves you with a void you need to fill. You hear people say it about musicians and comedians, that you try and chase the high, and players are the same. The money that players spend on cars or watches or putting diamonds on things that don't really need diamonds on them can be a way of trying to match the feeling that comes from winning.

But it is after disappointment that you most need a way to make yourself feel better. More than that, it's after a disappointment that was your fault. As an individual, knowing that it was your error that cost your team a win, or a point, eats you up. It haunts you. It preys on your mind, for days or for weeks. You know that your team-mates blame you and you know they're right, because you blame yourself, too.

I was low after that Chelsea game. It was humiliating. But I don't think I've ever been as down as I was after the Manchester derby a couple of years later, the day we lost 4–3 at Old Trafford. No game has ever hurt me as much as that one. The mistake that I made stayed with me longer than anything else. It still hurts now.

It's not immediately obvious that the winning goal – scored by Michael Owen in the sixth minute of injury time – was my fault. You might even assume that Shaun Wright-Phillips was to blame, given that I'm standing there, pointing at him, doing everything I can to make sure everyone thinks he was the one who let Owen have a free run at goal. But I was only doing that because I knew, deep down, that it was all on me.

I was playing right-back, with Kolo Touré and Joleon Lescott in central defence, but as the game wore on I'd drifted further and further inside. It's a form of cheating: I was leaving Shaun to deal with Patrice Evra and Ryan Giggs and using Kolo and Joleon as a bit of a crutch. There was safety in the middle, safety in numbers. It was much easier to be there, 'helping' them out, than all on my own out on the flank, trying to cover two of the best wide play-ers English football has ever seen.

The problem, obviously, was that there was now a vast area of the pitch totally unoccupied, deep into injury time in a finely poised Manchester derby. Shaun was sprinting back as fast as he could to try to cover the ground, but it was a thankless task. He was quick, Shaun, but nobody is quite that quick. We'd fought back from a goal down three times by that stage and should really have been about to pick up a valuable point at the home of our fiercest rivals. It would have been a bit of a watershed result. That was the first year that City were expected to challenge for the title, and this was our chance to prove that we were United's equals.

We almost managed it, too. If only someone hadn't abandoned their position, leaving Michael Owen to hang out, completely unmarked, on the edge of the penalty area with just a few seconds to go. It was the worst feeling of my career. Which is strange, because it was definitely Shaun Wright-Phillips's fault. Why else would I have been pointing at him?

How bad I felt after that game was made worse by a little habit I'd picked up when I first came through. Players will always tell you that they don't read the papers, that they don't listen to the radio, that they don't watch the analysis of their performances on TV. Now that I'm on the other side, I can tell you for a fact that is not true. Everyone is well aware of what is being said about them. They see the responses they get on social media. They hear what pundits and commentators say about them.

When I broke into Manchester City's team, it was still pretty common to have newspapers in the changing room, or in the canteen at the training ground. We might not all have read every match report, but most of the time you'd have a little look to see what mark out of ten you'd been given from your last game. It wasn't just me doing it – it was completely normal for most of the squad. The problem was that I didn't just stop there. I didn't have a glance at the paper, see that I'd been given a seven or an eight or a nine and then leave it. That was just the gateway. I'd go out on a Sunday or a Monday and buy all the papers, checking what mark I'd been given in each one, but even that wasn't enough for me. So I went looking for the hard stuff. I started reading the comments.

You have to remember that I'd come through as the next big thing coming out of Manchester City's academy. The fans were going crazy at the prospect of having a genuine home-grown star on their hands. I was getting compared to anyone and everyone. I was being linked with moves left, right and centre. It would be Chelsea one week, Manchester United the next, Real Madrid the week after that. I was on fire: a regular in the first team, and then the youngest ever defender to play for England. I could do no wrong. If City lost, as we did quite a lot back then, I was spared the worst of the criticism. The rest of the team wasn't good enough for me, I was being let down by my teammates, I was thriving despite being trapped in a fairly average side. I'd be lying if I said that I didn't love every bit of it.

That led me on to look for more. As well as reading the ratings in the *Manchester Evening News* and the *Daily Mail* and the *Sun* and everything else, I started to trawl through the comments. There would be dozens, hundreds of them underneath, and most of them were pretty positive, too. Being young helps, of course – fans are pretty forgiving of inexperienced players. They're willing to overlook the mistakes that you make. You're young. You'll learn. And everyone wanted me to do well, as a kid from the academy, as the new superstar that represented the future of the club. It adds an extra little spring to your step. I was confident anyway, but knowing all of these people think you're great, too? It makes you feel invincible.

It was the worst mistake I ever made, because at some point, as they were always going to, things started to turn. And when they did, boy did they turn. First it was with City. There was a perception that I was playing well for England, but that my form had dipped for City. I wasn't marauding like I used to. I didn't score enough goals, even if nobody seemed very sure about exactly how many goals the right-back should be scoring. I didn't get enough assists, either. Nobody seemed to stop to think that maybe I was playing with a better quality of players for England than I was for Manchester City, or that you get more chances to maraud when you're playing against Estonia or Andorra than you do against Manchester United or Chelsea. What mattered was that my performances for my club had slipped once I'd become an international. I must have gone big-time. I must have had my head turned by someone else. I must not be trying hard enough.

Then it started to happen with England, too. I remember reading the comments after the Croatia game at Wembley, the one that cost us a place at Euro 2008, me £1.5 million and Steve McClaren his job. I'd thought I'd played all right that night, even if the performance as a whole wasn't good enough. It wasn't a vintage display or anything, but I'd done my job. And then I opened one paper to see that I'd been given a three out of ten. A three! The comments were the same. All of a sudden, I wasn't the bright new thing anymore. I was still in my teens, but I was already being told that I wasn't good enough, that I wasn't up to scratch, that England needed to find a better right-back if they were going to recover from the humiliation of not qualifying for the European Championship.

It was made worse by the fact that, a few weeks later, I made a mistake away from the pitch, one that ended up in the papers. I was caught with a girl, and although the story as it appeared wasn't quite accurate, the damage was done. It led to me getting dropped from the England squad. Fabio Capello, who had just been installed as manager, said it was unacceptable. Because of the failure to get to the Euros, the mood around England was dark. The players were seen as spoiled brats, mollycoddled millionaires despite not even being good enough to qualify for a tournament. I was cast as typical of that: entitled and arrogant and waltzing round Manchester, dressed up as a rap star. It was my mistake and I have to own it, but the timing was bad, too. It meant I was portrayed in a particular light, one that was not very flattering at all. I was no longer the next big thing. Now I was an example of everything that was wrong with English football. People didn't want me to do well anymore. They wanted me to fail.

Just as all of these people building you up make you feel like you can take on the world, it's impossible not to suffer when you know that everyone has decided that actually you're a bit crap. You try to shake it off, to tell yourself that they don't know what they're talking about, but it's hard not to lose a bit of confidence, to find all that swagger that you need to succeed on the pitch starting to disappear, to feel like maybe you've been found out, to wonder if you might just have been dreadful all along. There's a reason why they tell you not to read the comments. Nothing good can ever be found below the line.

The next time I did get called up for England, once Capello had allowed me back into the fold so that he could make my life a misery in training, Lampard was in the squad, too. I was more nervous of seeing him than anyone else. I wondered if he'd remember the little encounter we'd had at Stamford Bridge. What if he told me that it was unacceptable to smash into a fellow England player? What if he was angry? Or what if he decided he wanted to gloat, to make it clear that he'd put the cocky upstart in his place? What if he remembered that I'd somehow managed to be responsible for conceding six goals in a single game?

He did remember, as it turned out. The first time we saw each other, he made a beeline for me. My heart was pounding. This was it. He stretched out his hand and shook mine. 'I'm one of the good guys,' he said, with a big smile on his face. He hadn't ignored me because he'd forgotten who I was, or because he thought he was better than me. Frank is quite shy. He's naturally kind of reserved. He keeps himself to himself. Before games, he goes quiet because that's him getting into his zone, getting himself mentally ready to play. It's how he deals with that pressure. It wasn't arrogance. I'd misread the situation completely. It taught me a lesson. No matter how well you think you know someone, you can never be entirely sure what's going on inside their head.

11
FRANCK RIBÉRY IS LAUGHING AT ME

The worst place to finish in the league is fifth. Or maybe sixth. Or it could be seventh, depending on who wins the Cup. They all have the exact same drawback. They all mean that you have the least wanted prize in football: a place in the Europa League.

There's nothing wrong with the Europa League as a competition. It's quite good, once it gets going. In my season on loan at Fiorentina, we went as far as the semi-finals, and the knockout stages were full of exactly the sorts of games that you associate with European football. We were drawn against Tottenham first, in the round of 32. I was desperate to play in those games, to show the Premier League what it was missing, to prove that I wasn't finished, to remind England and English football exactly who I was. Obviously, that meant I was injured for the first game. We drew 1–1 at White Hart Lane, but I did everything I could to be ready the following week, for the return game at the Artemio Franchi. I made it, too, and it was everything I wanted: we absolutely battered them, made it through to the next round, and the Curva, where the hardcore fans sit, was deafening at the final whistle. We got Roma in the last 16 and scored three goals in about 20 minutes in Rome to make it to the quarter-finals. Then we beat Dynamo Kyiv easily, and all of a sudden we were in a major semi-final, a couple of steps away from a trophy. Sadly, we ran into the one team you really don't want to play in the Europa League: Sevilla. Nobody wins the Europa League more than Sevilla. If they're in it, there's no point anyone else turning up. They hammered us, home and away, and we were out, but at least we'd been put out by a proper team.

No, the problem with the Europa League is that it ruins your plans. From a player's point of view, playing one game a week is a dream. Your body gets to rest and recover after every weekend. You get proper training sessions. You can prepare for the next opponent properly, make sure your head is right. Also, and this is a minor thing, you have a chance to have a nice and busy social life. You can go out after a game on a Saturday. You might go out on a Sunday, too: Monday, normally, would be a day off, so you didn't have to worry about training. You might pop out on a Tuesday, too, or a Wednesday. You had time. There was no pressure.

The Europa League ruins all that. Suddenly, everything becomes very serious. It's a hindrance. You play league games on a Sunday. You can't go out for 48 hours before a game, which rules out Friday and Saturday, and most of the time you can't go out afterwards, because you're travelling back. Tuesday and Wednesday are gone, too, because of having to travel across Europe to get to your next fixture. It messes up the whole routine, and in the group stages, it messes it up for games against teams that are not exactly the ones you grew up dreaming of playing against.

I don't want to be disrespectful. I don't want fans thinking that I'd forgotten where I'd come from, or where Manchester City had come from. I know that, to a lot of people, the fact that less than 20 years after City had been playing in League One they got to go on European trips to Poland and to Denmark and to everywhere else was a dream come true. It was a sign of how far the club had come. For a lot of them, it was a new experience, and they relished it. But I want to be honest, too. And if I'm honest, I had no idea where Lech Poznan was. Not a Scooby Doo.

The same goes for teams like Aalborg, and Streymur, and Omonia Nicosia, who we played in the seasons we qualified for the Europa League. For fans, these are romantic trips. They're an adventure, a chance to follow their team abroad, to discover new cities and countries. For players, there is absolutely nothing to be gained. You're used to playing against Cristiano Ronaldo in the Premier League and now someone's telling you that you're spending your week going to Poznan, you'll be playing in front of 5,000 people and, oh, if you don't win you'll be told you're a laughing stock.

Preparation for these games would be minimal. There's no detailed analysis of what you need to do, not even what you'd get ahead of a bog-standard Premier League game.

Even the managers don't take those early games all that seriously. Look at Brendan Rodgers: before Leicester City qualified for the Europa Conference League, the knock-off Nigel Europa League, he didn't even know what it was. He had no idea Leicester could even play in it, or at least he didn't until they got to the semi-finals. If that's what the manager thinks, the players don't stand a chance. You'd have a 10-minute meeting beforehand – 10 minutes at the absolute maximum – and every single player would be sitting there thinking: 'Oh yeah, we'll beat these.'

You can see how much they've been paying attention from the press conferences. They'll be asked an earnest question about what they make of the opposition. Who's the star man? 'We don't want to single out an individual,' they answer. 'They're a good team, and everyone is a threat.' That's code for: 'I don't know any of their names, and wasn't really listening when the manager told me.' That isn't the way it should be, obviously. But that is how players think; I definitely wasn't unique in finding the Europa League a bit of an afterthought. It's not all that surprising that English teams quite often come unstuck in the Europa League. A lot of the time, the teams you're playing are pretty useful. But the assumption is always that you're a Premier League player in a Premier League team, so it will be no problem at all.

There's so much confidence, in fact, that we'd regularly get on the plane and have absolutely no idea where we were going. There might be a couple of players who took an interest, and of course occasionally there was someone who was going back to their homeland, so felt it was special, but for most of us it was just another trip, just another game. It was only when we were in the air that someone would think to ask where we would be landing, and some long-suffering staff member would have to point out that Poznan is, in fact, in Poland. Though even they might be a little bit vague about where exactly in Poland it was.

If that sounds ridiculous, remember that players do not really have to think about travel. They're not booking flights and checking hotels and seeing what there is to do in a city. You don't even have to pack. The club takes care of all that. All you have to do is download whatever films or games you want for the flight onto your iPad or your laptop – I was a *Football Manager* player, every squad has a few – and make sure you have a pair of boxers. You go to the airport with nothing more than your washbag. Those bags are, like everything else, a source of fierce competition. First, it had to be Louis Vuitton. Then, it was Gucci. After a while, they had to be monogrammed, your initials stitched into them. It's the same with what's inside. Players aren't carrying Dove or Nivea or Sure deodorant. It'll be some designer one, the one that's the must-have designer deodorant at any given time. You'd want to have some aftershave, too, and your wallet, though you probably wouldn't have much chance to use it. Sometimes, players would take a washbag with abso-lutely nothing in, not even a bottle of ketchup. It was purely and simply because they knew they had to carry one. It was a crucial accessory. It was how everyone knew you were a footballer. That was all they needed to take:

an empty bag. The club packs all of the kit, your training gear, your boots. Everything else is taken care of for you. You're only meant to be thinking about football, not whether you might need a jumper in the evenings, or where Poznan is.

The most a player has to do is hand their passport in at the front desk before training the day they're due to travel, and the club takes it from there. Sometimes, even that was too much. There would always be one player who would somehow manage to leave their passport at home, even if the staff had made a point of telling them before they left the previous day and they'd been reminded on the group chat that morning that they had to bring it in. But even that is not your problem: the club would dispatch a driver to your house and they'd go and collect it for you, so you were in plenty of time to make the coach to the private terminal at the airport. One or two players I knew were so bad at remembering their passports that they had special rules in place: they had to bring their passports in two or three days beforehand, because it was so predictable that they'd forget.

It's the same when you land in a city. You're ferried from the airport straight to the hotel. You might go and have a training session at the stadium, partly to get used to the pitch and the stands and the sight lines, but mainly because UEFA used to tell the club that they had to. Then you'd go back to the hotel, have a bite to eat, get a massage, and then go to your room. You weren't allowed to leave. You couldn't go and do a bit of sightseeing, even if you wanted to. The most fresh air you'd get would be a

10-minute walk around the hotel the day of the game. I have no idea who came up with that, but it has to be the most pointless tradition in football. The idea is to get some air in your lungs, to stretch your legs, but I'm not sure how fresh the air is in a hotel car park, and I can stretch in my room. The walk does absolutely nothing. You don't even get to see the city. The most human contact you get is with fans hunting autographs, and even that can be a bit of an anticlimax. I'm happy to sign anything for anyone, but even I couldn't help noticing that a lot of the faces started to look familiar after a while. The same person I signed 20 things for two weeks ago was in front of me with another 20 things for me to sign. They'd assure you they weren't selling them off, but it wasn't exactly convincing. Where are you putting all this stuff? What are you doing with it?

No, on European trips, where you are is completely irrelevant. Everywhere looks the same, when all you see is a landing strip, a stadium, a hotel, and a bit of its car park. There's no incentive to learn where Poznan is. You won't see any of it, anyway.

That changes when you're in the Champions League. Everyone sits a little higher in their seats. Everyone pays a little more attention in meetings. Everyone forgets that they're missing out on a big Tuesday night out. To most players, Europe means the Champions League. The Champions League is a genuine prize. Not so much because of the cities – you still don't get to see any of them – but because of the stadiums. The Bernabéu, Camp Nou, the Allianz Arena: they're the most iconic stadiums in the world. They're the ones where you prove that you can live with the very highest level of football imaginable. The Champions League is where you get the recognition that you belong among the best on the planet. You want to be a footballer in the first place because of the chance to play in games, to be part of occasions, like these.

There were a couple of exceptions – I'm not sure Carlos Tevez was ever fazed by anything, he could be playing at Real Madrid and it would be like a normal day for him – but for most of us, those stadiums were special. We played at some incredible places in those first few years in the Champions League at Manchester City. We went to Borussia Dortmund and to Bayern Munich and to Barcelona. People like Vincent Kompany, Pablo Zabaleta and Joe Hart would be captivated by the idea of playing there; they wanted to know what it felt like to walk out on that pitch, to hear the crowd, to see the stands. They were the more studious sorts of players, but the effect of the Champions League was not limited to them.

Mario Balotelli was not the sort to be affected by where he was playing, but even he was sufficiently intimidated by a trip to Napoli to warn us all about what to expect beforehand. It was only when we arrived in Naples that we realised just how famous he was, at that point, back in Italy. We'd known he was high-profile, of course, and he'd already become a bit of a staple of the tabloids because, well, things tended to happen when Mario was around, but in Italy it was another level entirely. There were thousands of fans outside the team's hotel, not in the slightest bit interested in Sergio or Yaya or even me, but all of them desperate for a glimpse of Mario. They loved him in Italy. Or at least I think they loved him. I never really stopped to find out why they were outside our hotel.

There was definitely no affection once we got to the stadium. The San Paolo – now renamed the Diego Armando Maradona Stadium – is a bit of a ruin, but it is probably the most hostile place I've ever played. You could feel it even before you'd stepped off the bus. The drive there felt like going through a war zone. Inside, the changing rooms were nothing like we were used to from the Premier League. There's a moat around the pitch. It's like it has all been designed to make you want to leave as quickly as possible, and not do anything as stupid as upsetting the locals.

Balotelli had known what was coming – he'd played there for Inter Milan – and he'd done what he could to make sure we were prepared. 'This is not a place to fuck around,' he'd said. It was the one stadium where even he felt a little unsettled. Napoli had a good side, then, with Marek Hamšík, Ezequiel Lavezzi and Edinson Cavani, but their main weapon wasn't just the crowd, but the stadium itself. 'These players don't mess about,' he said. 'If you give them a chance, they'll take it. They're killers.' He was right. We lost that night. I've never heard a noise like it.

That is the key with the Champions League: you have to be ready. If you're not fully prepared, you'll be exposed in a second. My first appearance in the Champions League is the only time I ever felt truly out of my depth. It was the only time in my entire career when I started to think that maybe the level was too high for me.

In my defence, it was as tough a start as you could imagine: away at the Allianz Arena against Bayern Munich. Not just any Bayern Munich: the Bayern Munich of Franck Ribéry, Philipp Lahm, Toni Kroos and Thomas Müller. I hadn't been expecting to play. Roberto Mancini, our manager, had told me that he was planning on using Zabaleta, but then he changed his mind at the last minute. He thought my pace might be a better bet against Ribéry, Bayern's star winger. The problem is that you need to know if you're starting or not. I used to watch all the clips of my direct opponent that I could get my hands on in the couple of days before a game, so that I could work out what I would do when I came up against him. That way, I'd know what he was likely to do in certain situations, and I could come up with ways of stopping him. Ribéry had a signature move: he would go on his left, do some mad skill, and then chop inside, before whipping the ball with his right foot towards the far corner. The only way to handle that is not to commit in the challenge. You know the chop is coming, so you hold off for as long as you can.

I knew that, of course – it's Franck Ribéry, he's not exactly a mystery – but because I hadn't had a chance to do my research, I went into the game feeling a little bit under-prepared.

It didn't help that I was out on the pitch beforehand and saw him giggling with my teammate Samir Nasri. They knew each other from the French national team; they'd both come through at Marseille. They were mates. But I also knew that Ribéry had texted Nasri the night before and asked him who he thought might play at right-back for us. Nasri hadn't given anything away; he'd said it might be me because of my pace, but that he wasn't sure. Ribéry had sent a bit of harmless banter back in response: 'Tell Richards I'm going to destroy him,' something like that.

Now there they were, thick as thieves, whispering to each other and laughing. I'm not an insecure person. It takes a lot to knock my confidence. I don't speak French. But a few minutes before I made my debut in the Champions League, for some reason I was absolutely certain they were laughing about me. All sorts of scenes ran through my head. Ribéry had been watching my highlights and he couldn't believe how bad I was. He was telling Nasri he couldn't believe that I was a professional. And Nasri was joining in! It never occurred to me that they were probably talking about something completely unrelated. It is, after all, somehow possible that the first thing two old friends talked about when they saw each other was not the relative ability of Micah Richards. All I knew was that, all of a sudden, I didn't want to play. Drop me for Zabaleta. Let him deal with this. I'd seen Ribéry ending careers, and I didn't want him to do it to me. My confidence was completely shot, and we hadn't even finished warming up yet.

The game played out just as I'd expected. Ribéry took me to pieces. I couldn't get close to him that night. I touched the ball about eight times. Most of them were tackles. Desperate, last-ditch slide tackles after he'd gone past me again. I was so busy trying not to be humiliated that I barely noticed the kerfuffle on the touchline. There was lots of shouting, lots of swearing, lots of arms swinging about wildly.

That wasn't, admittedly, that unusual under Roberto Mancini. He could be – I'll put this delicately – quite emotional, as a manager. He used to lose his mind at absolutely everybody. He would go nuts with me, on average, about eight times a game. There was nothing strange about his prowling around the technical area, muttering under his breath, shaking his head, and then stomping over to the bench to give someone an earful.

Even from the pitch, though, even with Franck Ribéry ripping me apart, I knew this one was a bit different. When we got into the dressing room after the game – which we lost – it turned out that Carlos Tevez had refused to come on as a substitute. Mancini was shouting. Carlos was shouting. That was the good thing about Carlos: he really didn't care the slightest bit about who he was arguing with. If he felt he'd been wronged, he'd go for you. There was a league game when he fell out with Kompany once. Kompany had criticised him for something on the pitch, and when they got back into the dressing room there'd been an almighty row. It had looked, at one point, like they might come to blows, so me and Joleon and a couple of the other big lads had taken it on ourselves to hold Vincent back, to stop him attacking Carlos. We stood in front of him, blocking his path, holding his arms. It was at that point that Carlos noticed Vincent was basically powerless, so he walked up to him and cracked him in the face. We'd accidentally given Carlos a free hit on his own captain. Kompany was fuming afterwards. Not with

Carlos; by that stage, he'd decided that part was quite funny. He was steaming with me and Joleon for restraining him so he couldn't get out of the way. He couldn't even fall over. We were too busy holding him up.

It was the same in Munich. Carlos wasn't the sort to back down. He was shouting at Mancini. Mancini shouted back at him. A load of other players were joining in to have a go at Mancini. They were shouting, too. Half of us didn't really know what any of it was about, and we weren't overly concerned by it. The way it was presented later, as Tevez's 'mutiny in Munich', always seemed a bit overplayed to me. It was treated as though it was some massive falling out. It wasn't. Mancini fell out with everyone almost all of the time. It was just another Tuesday.

Really, I should be quite thankful to Carlos. His showdown with the manager meant that nobody was in the least bit interested in my own performance. For the first time in my career, I came away from Munich not entirely sure whether I was good enough to be on that pitch. It was the sort of experience I'd always craved – the Allianz rocking, the stadium lit up in Bayern's colours, up against one of the best teams in the world – but as Ribéry danced past me again and again, and City lost comfortably, I felt like maybe it was a step too far for me. I'd always been one of the best players on any team I'd been in. I'd been able to step up to every challenge I'd faced. I'd never been fazed by anything. If this was what elite looked like, though, I started to wonder if I'd reached my limit. I'd always assumed this was where I belonged, but now had to ask myself if I was good enough.

That psychological side is incredibly important in the Champions League in particular. I've never really suffered from nerves. When I was younger, I was basically fearless. Nothing threw me. But in the Champions League, you're so aware of the level of player you're facing that nearly anything can throw you. You can almost become paranoid.

I remember going to play Ajax at the Amsterdam ArenA in our second season in the Champions League. We were a little more experienced then, and even though there is no more famous name in European football than Ajax, as a team competing for the Premier League title, we were expecting to win. A few minutes before the game, I saw one of the Ajax coaches pull Patrick Vieira aside. And not just any coach: it was Patrick's old teammate from Arsenal, Dennis Bergkamp. This time, I was close enough to hear exactly what was being said. Bergkamp asked Vieira who was playing at right-back. This wasn't the same as Ribéry trying to find out from Nasri who he might be up against. This was just before the game: Ajax would have seen our team sheet. He'd seen exactly who was playing at right-back. He just hadn't heard of me. They'd obviously been expecting Zabaleta to start the game and assumed that I was some kid who'd been drafted in. It cut me deep. I'd been in the team for years! I was a mainstay of the side! I was an England international! But still Dennis Bergkamp had no idea who I was. Vieira didn't know I was listening, but fortunately for my fragile state of mind, he backed me up. 'No, no, this is the one,' he said. 'You can't get past him.' That made me feel a bit better, but to an extent the damage was done. I'd been dismissed by Ajax before they'd even seen me play. My confidence had been sky high, and now it was plummeting through the floor. I'd love to say I proved everyone wrong. I didn't. We lost that night, too. It turned out that Vieira wasn't quite right. You could get past me. And the rest of the City team, for that matter.

That's what sets the Champions League apart. The Premier League is relentless, but occasionally the technical level isn't the highest. Players make mistakes. They make the wrong choices. Most of the time, or at least some of the time, you get a chance to make up for whatever errors you've made. You can run back into position, cover lost ground, or at least hope that the cross or the shot isn't up to much.

The technical level in international football, on the other hand, is far higher, but the game itself is a lot slower. I made my debut for England against Holland – I don't know if I've mentioned it, but I was the youngest defender ever to represent the national team – and was up against a Bayern Munich player that day, too: Arjen Robben. He was just as draining an opponent as Ribéry, but the more cautious style meant that he did not have quite as many chances to go one-on-one against me. I never really felt isolated: I had a winger supporting me, tracking a full-back, and more time to regroup, to make sure my positioning was right. You get a bit more help when you're playing for your country.

The Champions League combines the best – or the worst, depending on which way you're looking at it – of both. It's fast, and it's perfect. That's not just when you're facing the very best teams, the ones that are fancied to win it, but almost anybody. That Ajax team was top class. We couldn't get close to them, either, and they weren't expected to go far. In the Champions League, any team can hurt you at any time. The attacks keep coming. They do not stop. Any mistake at all can be fatal. The level is so high that if you slip up, you can be pretty sure your opponent won't.

Occasionally, that means playing in it isn't quite as appealing as it ought to be. Through my career, there was only one time I was glad not to be in the team. Normally, all I wanted to do was play. I was angry and frustrated whenever I was dropped, even if it was to rest me for games to come. I knew that there was always a chance that I wouldn't get my place back if I gave it up even briefly, because my rival for the position, Pablo Zabaleta, was so good. But when Manuel Pellegrini took me aside and told me he was going to start Zabaleta against Barcelona at Camp Nou, I wasn't quite as disappointed as he might have been expecting. It had been bad enough facing Franck Ribéry at the Allianz. It's no fun playing against opponents of Barca's quality. You barely touch the ball. You don't get to express yourself. You worry beforehand that they're giggling about you with your teammates. You spend your evening running behind them, doing your best to keep up. Playing against Lionel Messi would be one of those once-in-a-lifetime experiences. But to be honest, that sounded like once too many to me.

Even Pellegrini knew there was no way to stop Messi. He didn't pretend he had some masterplan to shut him down, or that he'd spotted some flaw in his game that we could exploit. The problem is that Messi doesn't really play in a position. He spends the first few minutes of every game walking around, sizing up the pitch, checking to see where the spaces and the gaps and the opportunities might be. Once he's made his mind up, he spends the entire game exploiting them. You can't tell one player to mark him, because he'll take that player on a tour of the whole pitch. He'll wreck your shape. He does his damage by taking you into places that you don't want to go, finding space anyway, and then getting on the half-turn and driving at you. And once he's doing that, it only tends to end one way: with you doing your best impression of Jerome Boateng, falling to the ground as Messi darts past. The only option you have, really, is the one that Pellegrini came up with: sheer quantity. You have to try to swarm Messi with numbers. Even that probably won't work, but it's your only choice.

I didn't mind when Pellegrini told me that Zabaleta would be the one having to deal with all of that. Having the chance to watch Messi, up close and personal from the substitutes' bench, seemed like enough of a privilege to me. These are the games that inspired you to put in all of that hard work to become a professional. They're the games that define your career. It's the Champions League. It's the ultimate test. It's the best players on the planet. They're the games you want to be part of, more than anything. But sometimes, being a substitute is as close as you want to get.

12

TIM SHERWOOD'S SEDUCTION TECHNIQUE

There are a surprising number of similarities between being a footballer on the verge of moving clubs and having an affair. I imagine. Both situations involve a lot of secretive telephone calls. Both require you to sneak into hotel rooms using a fake name. Both take up a lot of your spare time. And both tend to end with an older man telling you exactly where you've gone wrong.

I'm not entirely sure why everyone involved in transfers is still so wedded to booking hotel rooms. Obviously, you can't hold a clandestine – and illegal, at least as far as football is concerned – meeting at a training ground, or a stadium. A player with a contract at one club can't just turn up for a job interview at another. It doesn't work like that. It's too obvious. You couldn't go to a manager's house, either. Everyone has at least one nosy neighbour, a curtain-twitcher, who would be straight on the phone. That's the last thing you need, when you're trying to keep things hush-hush. I can see why everything has moved on from service stations, too. That's where they did their business in the

1980s, but now it would feel a bit seedy. It's a public place, for a start: that's not ideal. Also, you'd be surprised at how few footballers you see at the Costa Coffee at Leigh Delamere. You could do everything remotely, on Skype or Zoom or something, but a lot of managers like to do things face to face. Maybe they just like the thrill of the secrecy.

Most likely, it's to do with keeping the loop closed. Sometimes, only a handful of people in the world will know that meeting is happening. Four is probably the minimum: the manager and the player, and both of their agents. That means if it leaks, they can limit the number of suspects. Or they could, if they didn't insist on meeting in hotels. That automatically means the list of possible moles grows considerably: the manager, the player, both of their agents, and literally every person who works in the hotel.

No matter how well you try to hide the fact that you've booked a room to have a clandestine meeting – the manager and the player arriving separately, the room being booked in an agent's name – you still have to walk through reception. You can still see at least one member of staff thinking: 'Oh, that's interesting, both of those people I recognise have walked through the lobby within ten minutes of each other, both have gone immediately to the lifts, and neither of them are actually booked in to stay here.' You can practically see them scrabbling off to tell all of their colleagues, or reaching for their phone to text their mates. There must be so many stories about transfers that are leaked because the meeting has been held at a hotel. Have agents not heard of serviced apartments? It might save a bit of money, as well as embarrassment.

These meetings are just plain weird. The year before I left Manchester City, word got back to me that a couple of Premier League teams were interested in signing me. I hadn't played much the previous season, 2013–14. Pablo Zabaleta was, by that stage, very clearly City's first-choice right-back, despite all the time I'd spent telling people that he was too slow. I'd found it quite frustrating. When we won the Premier League, and I had to go on the pitch despite not having played enough games to get a medal, that turned into something close to humiliation. I was ready to think about moving on.

Eventually, my agent persuaded me that the best thing to do would be to meet with one of the managers who wanted to sign me. Now strictly speaking that isn't allowed: it's what's known in football as 'tapping up', but it's always seemed to me to be an extremely old-fashioned rule. If you have a contract with your employer, then of course you're allowed to go and meet another one, to find out if they might have a better job to offer you, or be willing to pay you more, or want to give you the nice corner office, the one with the spectacular view. I don't really see why football should be any different, especially in cases like that, when it was perfectly clear to everyone that I wasn't in City's plans anymore.

I didn't like breaking the rules, particularly, and I wasn't entirely sure what he was going to tell me. What mattered was whether anyone could make a bid that would tempt City to sell. Nothing that a manager could say to me about how his team played, or how he wanted to use me, would matter until an offer had been accepted.

The idea of going to meet him struck me as incredibly awkward.

At the time, though, I could read the writing on the wall. I wasn't playing. The club clearly didn't care whether I stayed or not. I felt a little like I was in the last chance saloon. I knew I needed to go somewhere else, and it made sense to find out where might be the best fit for me. I felt a little honour-bound, too: it would have been seen as a bit of a snub if I'd just declared that I didn't want to go and meet a manager. So I decided, a little reluctantly, that I'd probably better go.

We arranged to meet in a hotel one afternoon. He went in first, and I followed a few minutes later, slipping into the room as subtly as a man of my size and dress sense can. This was his chance to persuade me that my future lay with him, that he could help me fulfil all of my ambitions, that he was the man that I should have been with all along. He started that process by shaking my hand, looking me in the eye and saying: 'What the fuck has happened to you?'

There was no messing about. No dinner and drinks beforehand to try and get me in the mood. He was straight down to business, telling me exactly how crap he thought I was. 'I thought you were going to be the next Cafu,' he said. 'But you've stopped doing the basics of the game. Nobody can get past you. You can overlap. So why aren't you doing it?'

I stammered something about injuries, about having to play at centre-back, about not getting a run in the team, but he wasn't having any of it. 'Don't give me excuses.

Playing in the middle should be easy for you. You've just been a bit shit.'

That was his pitch. I was in the room for an hour or so, and he spent a decent portion of it insulting me. The thing is, though, I loved it. All any player wants is a manager to be honest with them. You have enough people around you telling you how great you are; after a while, you can't really be sure which bits are sincere and which bits are just buttering you up.

I knew, obviously, that he didn't think I was all that bad: why would he be considering spending £20 million of someone else's money to sign me if he thought I was a waste of space? But if he thought I wasn't doing all I could, that was fine. How was he going to make me better? 'Don't worry,' he said. 'I'll get you playing again.' He didn't give me any detailed answers, not really. We didn't go into heat maps or tactical plans or his philosophy. He didn't try to overload me with information.

That move didn't work out. I never really found out why. Maybe the club thought that City's asking price was a bit too steep. Maybe someone looked at one of my knees. Maybe City decided, late on, that they didn't want to sell me to a team that could, in theory, challenge them for the Premier League title. Maybe he had never really wanted to sign me: he just wanted to get me into a hotel room to tell me how terrible he thought I was. Maybe I was meant to buy him dinner. Whatever it was, I ended up spending the last year of my contract at City out on loan in Italy, with Fiorentina, and then had to face the prospect of finding another club again.

It is easier to do that when you're soon to be out of contract. Then, you're allowed to talk to anyone, and you can sign a deal with a team abroad six months in advance. I was flattered to have quite a few options. There was a three-year deal on the table at Fiorentina, turning my loan spell into a permanent stay. Bournemouth were interested, too: Eddie Howe had been out to watch a training session at Fiorentina that season, just to get an idea of how the club worked, and he'd obviously realised that I was the key man.

West Ham came in for me, too, and had put the most money on the table: theirs was the most lucrative offer. The problem was that they were only prepared to put a two-year deal on the table. Aston Villa, on the other hand, wanted to pay me less, but to tie me down for four years. That security was really important to me, especially given the injury problems I'd had.

I had some links with Birmingham – I was born there, and still had relatives in the city – and my dad was convinced it was a bit of a sign, so I thought I'd better at least talk to Tim Sherwood, the manager, to see how he thought it would work, what his plans were. We did that one over the phone.

His first words were just what any player wants to hear: 'Fucking hell, if I'd only been watching you for the last six months, I wouldn't be signing you. And you're a bit heavy these days.' He had exactly the same delicate, affectionate seduction technique as the other manager I'd met. I'd assumed he'd want to try to sell Aston Villa to me, to walk through his vision for the team, to talk about the history of the club, the power of the Holte End, maybe even discuss whether he might want me to be his captain. They wanted to sign me, after all. They'd sought me out. But no, he wanted to spend a good half-hour slagging me off, and then the other half-hour telling me how he'd make me a better player.

You leave those conversations with your self-confidence in tatters, but I always responded well to that. I like a bit of tough love. I want that brutal honesty. If that's what you genuinely think, if that's what you really believe, then I appreciate you telling me. There isn't enough honesty in football, so any little bit you find is precious.

Pretty much every player spends their entire career surrounded by transfers, or at least the possibility of a transfer. Most of the time, they will not have the slightest clue what's going on with their own careers. They will be told one thing by their agent, one thing by their club, and a dozen other things by a dozen other people. Most of the time, when you call the people who are meant to be looking after you, it's to try to find out what is going on. That can be when you've heard someone is interested in you, and you want to get to the bottom of it. It can be because you know that a bid has gone in, and you want to see if there's any progress. In those situations, you bombard your agent: they're busy trying to finalise contracts and signing-on fees and play peacemaker with the clubs and make sure their fees and their cut is safe, and you're calling them every day, twice a day, three times a day for updates. You know full well, deep down, that there's nothing they can tell you, because if there was any news that was worth passing on, they would do it, even if it was the most minor update. It's more for your own sanity. It's out of desperation, really. It's your career, your life that everyone is discussing, and you feel like it's being decided without you. It's all out of your hands. Quite a lot of the time, the player is the last person to find out what is actually happening.

The reason for this uncertainty is that the whole football industry runs on rumour and whisper. Most of that is powered by agents. Not your agent, necessarily: when things are going well, there are always agents knocking around, conspiring to do something. There are plenty of good agents, ones who look after their clients, ones who have their best interests at heart. But there are probably more who do not quite fit that description.

There are agents who will get word from a club that a certain player is on their list. Not on top of the list, not the absolute priority, but a player of interest. That agent will then call your agent and say that this club is thinking of signing you. The only way a deal can happen, though, will be if they're involved. This isn't an agent that represents you. It's not even officially an agent that represents a club. It's just an agent trying to insert themselves into the deal so that they can take a cut.

Naturally, your agent doesn't like the sound of that, so they'll ring the club direct and ask what's going on. Sometimes, that has the effect of cutting out the middleman; your agent might know someone there who can fill them in on the details, and see if there's any prospect of a deal going anywhere without the completely unnecessary complication of someone else taking a fee. At other times, the opposite happens. The club will say that they do want to sign a player, but that the only way a deal happens is if a specific agent is involved.

There are times, too, when it comes from within the dressing room. As a player, you do not know which deals are real and which are invented. You don't know when a club is seriously interested or when it's just agents trying to conjure a deal out of thin air, all in the hope of earning a commission. So you talk about it with the rest of the squad. Maybe one of your teammates goes back to their agent and asks if they've heard anything. That agent's eyes light up. The next thing you know, your teammate's agent is telling you that they've got a club interested in you, but the deal has to run through them. Now they're trying to insert themselves into the deal, trying to shape your future for their own interests.

There is a reason why, every transfer window, there are so many stories that lead to nothing. At times, maybe journalists do just make them up, but a lot of the time, they're just reflecting how chaotic everything is. There are loads of transfers that don't happen because the middleman can't get paid. And there are plenty more that happen only because they do get paid. Towards the end of my career, I was almost persuaded to move to Turkey. I'd just been relegated with Aston Villa, and Trabzonspor, one of the biggest clubs in the country, were interested. But I'd only been back in England for a year after leaving Fiorentina, and I'd just had a son. I didn't want to go abroad again. Besides, it felt as though Turkey was the sort of place that players went at the end of their careers. It was where you went to watch the sunset. I wasn't even 30 at that stage. I wasn't quite ready for that. The opportunity was pushed on me, though, because an agent was fishing for the juicy fee that would come with getting me to agree to move. A lot of transfers are like that: what a player wants is secondary. So is what is in the interests of any given club. It definitely was not in Trabzonspor's best interests to be signing me. What matters, often, is what works best for an agent.

Even now, I could not tell you what percentage of the transfer stories that centred on me during my career were actually true. In my first few years at Manchester City, I was linked with almost every club under the sun. Liverpool were in for me, supposedly. So were Arsenal, and Chelsea, and Tottenham, and Manchester United. Then there was Juventus, Napoli, Real Madrid and Bayern Munich.

I can say for certain that Chelsea's interest was genuine. Backed by Roman Abramovich's money, and inspired by José Mourinho's charisma, they were not just buying up superstars from abroad, but trying to corner the market for the best, young domestic talent. In the first summer of the Abramovich era, they'd signed Joe Cole, Glen Johnson and Wayne Bridge. A couple of years later, they'd raided City for Shaun Wright-Phillips, but Chelsea in those days didn't bother much with sentiment, or with patience. A couple of years later they'd made him available again. In fact, they'd even approached Manchester City with an idea. They wanted to send Shaun back to the Etihad in part-exchange for the next prodigy off the club's production line: me. They'd even throw some cash in as well. The whole deal would have been worth about £20 million. The club were tempted, but in the end I couldn't quite bring myself to do it.

I was still a kid, really. I loved my life in Manchester. I was living like a king. I was settled, and happy, and comfortable. Looking back, my career might have been very different if I'd had the nerve to go through with it. I might not have won a Premier League with Manchester City – and that, ultimately, meant more than anything – but the odds are I'd have got at least one with Chelsea. Maybe a Champions League, too. And while injuries were always my greatest issue, I do wonder if I might have benefited from being in a more elite environment earlier in my career, surrounded by players who would have pushed me on. I'm not sure being one of the best players at City, in the years before the takeover, was necessarily in my best interests. It allowed me to be a little complacent. I don't have regrets, not really, but I do wonder at times if I could have made more of my talent.

Aside from Chelsea, though, I have no idea how real any of those other deals were. That doesn't mean they don't put a bit of swagger in your step. It's hard not to walk into training with your shoulders back and your chest pumped out and a spring in your step when you've read that morning that Mourinho or Arsène Wenger or Alex Ferguson wants to spend tens of millions of pounds on you. It's the ultimate compliment, really. You want everyone to see the papers on those mornings. You're 19 or 20 and want everyone to know just who's watching you.

But football has a habit of giving with one hand and taking with the other. A year or so after I'd been linked with all of the great and the good of the Premier League, I was having a much rougher time. My form had dipped completely. For the first time in my career, I wasn't the boy wonder anymore. The takeover had happened, and there were endless rumours about City wanting to replace me with a variety of Brazilian full-backs.

Then, one morning, I saw my face on the back of one of the newspapers. The headline was: 'Taking the Mic'. Apparently City were now willing to cut their losses and sell me for as little as £5 million. That was bad. But it wasn't the worst bit. No, the worst bit was that Bolton and Wigan now felt that I was a realistic target. I was used to being linked with teams competing in the Champions League. Now I was on the verge of a move to Wigan?

When I pulled into training, I knew this would be a bit of a problem. We used to have all the newspapers out in the canteen. Anyone who had come in early to have their breakfast would already have seen it; once the session had ended and the whole squad marched up there for their lunch, the secret would definitely be out. I'd be a laughing stock. Bolton? Wigan? Instead of going straight for the dressing room, then, I made my way to the canteen. I swept up every single newspaper I could find, checked nobody was about, and went downstairs and crammed them all in my locker. Now nobody would find out that I was a 'realistic' target for Wigan. Not until they checked their phones, anyway.

Then Gelson Fernandes, a Swiss midfielder who had been at the club for a couple of years, appeared. I didn't know it, but apparently Gelson was a real news-hound. He probably had all sorts of alerts set up on his phone. Maybe he got all of the papers delivered. Whatever it was, he knew. Gelson read the papers. 'Have you seen who you've been linked with today?' he asked, all sweetness and innocence. And then he just started giggling. I could see why. It had all the key words. Micah Richards. Cut-price. Wigan.

Your teammates don't find every transfer rumour quite as funny as that. For years, Sergio Agüero would be linked with a move away from Manchester City to Barcelona, every summer. It made sense. Agüero was one of the best strikers in the world. He was also best mates with Lionel Messi; I think, as much as he loved City, there was always part of him that dreamed of being in the same club team together. Whenever the rumours started spreading, the rest of the players would plead with him not to go. You do whatever you can to pander to the ego, to convince them that this is where they belong. We'd beg him to stay. We'd tell him that he was the best player at the club. We'd suggest that he was better off out of Messi's shadow.

Others would get a different treatment. If there was someone in the dressing room who brought the vibe down, who was always negative, who didn't belong to any of the tribes, who seemed miserable despite being a rich, successful footballer, who didn't appear to be struggling with anything at home, then you'd be praying for someone to come and take them off your hands. They'd tell you they might be going, and it would be all you could do not to say: 'OK, don't let the door hit you on the way out.'

Even seeing players that you like, you respect, leave is not an especially emotional thing. I didn't really get a chance to say goodbye to City, despite being there since I was 14. I was on the pitch as we celebrated winning the Premier League in 2014, and then never played at the Etihad again. Clubs are much better now at giving long-serving players a proper send-off: look at the way that Fernandinho was treated when his contract expired. I got a few minutes in the Community Shield, and then just disappeared. I didn't really get a chance to say goodbye to my teammates, or to the staff, or even the fans. One day you're there, and the next day, you're not. There is no sentimentality.

Nigel de Jong had been a really important player for City in the first few seasons after the takeover. He was the sort of player you would want to go to war with, if you really had to go to war. He was good technically, but his main talent was making these impossible tackles. He had a snap and a snarl. He even managed to kick Xabi Alonso in the chest in the World Cup final in 2010 and somehow not get sent off. He had a real talent.

He was also one of my closest mates at the club. He was part of our little gang in the dressing room. We even lived next door to each other for a while. Smoke from his barbecue would drift over into my garden; footballs from my garden would fly over into his. We'd occasionally pop round to each other's houses and hang out. We even had our own personal boundary dispute. The two gardens were separated by a fence. Somehow, one of the panels had been knocked down. I hadn't done it, and I hadn't seen who'd done it. He said he hadn't done it, and hadn't seen who'd done it. So both of us refused to pay for it to be fixed. It wasn't so much the money – it would have been a few hundred quid to mend it, and we could both afford it – but the principle of the thing. I mean, given that we played football in my garden all of the time, it was probably one of my mates who had broken it, but I didn't know that. And without evidence, I wasn't prepared to admit my guilt.

Over the course of the season when we first won the title, though, it became more and more apparent that Nigel wasn't first choice anymore. We were basically playing with two midfielders, so that Roberto Mancini could accommodate two of Sergio Agüero, Carlos Tevez, Edin Džeko and Mario Balotelli up front. One of those midfielders, obviously, had to be Yaya Touré. We were, if you remember, 'shit without Yaya'. Even our manager thought that. Next to him, more and more, Mancini played Gareth Barry. You couldn't drop Barry because he did so much work; he was one of those players who you could only really appreciate when they weren't there. In the big games, certainly, they were first choice: Yaya and GB. That left Nigel as the fall guy.

He was never a hindrance. He never kicked up a fuss. It's in those moments that you find out who is a good professional, and Nigel was. But at the same time, he was starting to feel underappreciated. He wanted to play. He was too good not to be playing. He told me over and over again that he didn't want to leave, that he wanted to stay at City for as long as he could, that if he got the games then he would have no reason to go. The summer after we won the league, though, he realised that he did not really have a choice.

The first I knew of it was when he knocked on my door and told me that he was going. He didn't say where: as a rule, players are quite cautious about telling people that something is going to happen. You know well enough that nothing is certain until the ink is dry on every last piece of paper. It turned out he had an amazing opportunity: AC Milan had come in for him, and though they weren't quite what they had been a few years before, they were still a big, historic club with an iconic stadium in a major league. He would get the regular football that he wanted, and he'd be appreciated, too.

And that was that. By the time we gathered for pre-season again, Nigel just wasn't there anymore. I don't know if he'd told the rest of the squad, or even the players he was especially close to. Football is brutal like that. People just disappear from dressing rooms. The majority of transfers happen in the summer, when everyone is either away on holiday or at a major tournament. You come back and the whole dressing room can have changed. There aren't any leaving dos or big farewell speeches. You're just there one minute and gone the next. It happens every year, until it happens to you.

Sometimes, you miss them as players; if Sergio had gone to Barcelona in his prime, then we certainly would have missed him. But at a club like City, where you could be sure the manager was going out and signing a replacement who would probably be even better than the original, you miss them more as people.

It happened every year at City, back then. First it was Nigel. Then it was me. Then it was James Milner, and Joleon Lescott, and then Joe Hart. The club might have upgraded them as players, but you can't replace the character. These were the players who were the fabric of the dressing room. They were what held it together. And then, just like that, you don't see them again, and the next time you show up, the whole feel of the dressing room has changed. That was what happened with Nigel. We lost something when he left, off the pitch more than on it. Worst of all, he never did pay for that fence.

13

THE MICAH RICHARDS GUIDE TO LA DOLCE VITA

Sitting in a mid-range hotel in a city I didn't know, it felt like I'd made the biggest mistake of my life. Just a few weeks before, I'd been planning to spend my entire career at Manchester City. It was home. It had become one of the biggest clubs in the world in the time I'd been there, but it was where I felt comfortable. For years, my agent had had one of the easiest jobs in football: a renegotiation every few years, and then we all just got on with our lives.

This had started to change after we won the Premier League for the second time, in 2014. I'd played so little that season that I hadn't, technically, qualified to get a winners' medal. That summer, with a year to run on my current deal, the club approached me to talk about extending my contract. For the first time, I had doubts. I didn't want to be a mascot. I didn't want to spend the rest of my career on the bench, getting the occasional run-out in the Carabao Cup.

As much as anything, it was pride. I joke about bursting onto the scene now, but I didn't want my career to fizzle out. I'd started with a bang. I'd been the youngest defender to play for England. I'd been first choice in that first team of the new era at Manchester City, the one that won the FA Cup and ended the long wait for the title. It's probably pushing it to say I have a legacy at Manchester City – nobody's volunteering to build a statue of me outside the stadium – but I had been a part of that early success, and it meant a lot to me. I didn't want the second half of my career to be such an anticlimax, with me as an after-thought. I wanted to play.

City's offer was incredibly generous. Despite all of the injuries I'd had, they offered me a five-year deal. It was a lot of money. It would have looked after me for the rest of my career. It came with genuine emotion, too. Khaldoon al-Mubarak, the chairman, made a point of telling me that the club loved me, thought the world of me, wanted me to stay. He was fantastic with me. So were all of the other executives: Brian Marwood, Txiki Begiristain, Ferran Soriano. They said all of the things that you want to hear. They seemed sincere, and they put the club's money where their mouths were.

I couldn't shake that worry, though. Every club has to have a certain number of homegrown players: members of the squad who either came through at their academy or somewhere else in England. It's not many – eight out of 25 – but it's enough to be a factor when managers are thinking about how to build their teams, now that every major team has the pick of players from across the world. Most of the major teams, now, have a couple of players on the bench or in the squad who might have been sold if they didn't have a British passport. I didn't want to be one of those players. I didn't want to sign a contract to fulfil a quota.

Everyone around me told me to sign it. Joleon Lescott, who had been one of my closest friends at City, told me I was being stupid. If the worst came to the worst and I found that I just wasn't playing, he said, I could always go out on loan. That way I would still get the five-year deal, all the security, and there would be a way to guarantee I could still play football, too. The only problem with that logic was the quota: City would have to keep me around to make sure they had enough homegrown players in the squad. I'd be a tick in a box.

Eventually, with the summer passing by and the transfer deadline starting to hover, Manuel Pellegrini called me into his office. He needed to know, he said: was this all a bluff to get a better wage, or was I serious? Was I going to sign or not? If I didn't, he told me, he would have to go and find himself another back-up right-back, someone to keep Pablo Zabaleta on his toes. I had to give him an answer. I told him that I appreciated his honesty, how open he was being. He was a perfect gentleman, Pellegrini.

And then I told him I wasn't going to sign.

Almost as I said it, I thought to myself: there you go again, you and your big mouth. I hadn't ever thought of leaving City. I didn't have a plan. There was no better place for me: the physios and the medical staff had been looking after me since I was 14. Paul Kelly, Robin Sadler, Lee Nobes and Craig Yuill knew my knee inside out. Literally inside out, given how often I'd had it scanned. Sam Erith, Simon Bitcon, Tom Parry, Max Sala, James Baldwin, Mark

Sertori, Paul Webster and Ben Thompson were other members of the medical team that knew how to manage my body perfectly. They all knew what I could do and what I couldn't. They knew how to manage my workload. They'd taken brilliant care of me, and they'd almost certainly enabled me to play as much as I had. Leaving City, from the point of view of prolonging my career, was stupid. And I knew it.

At first, it seemed like everything might work out all right. There were a couple of English teams after me, including Tottenham. For a couple of weeks, that seemed like it might suit everyone. But an offer never arrived. There was a suggestion that City had decided they did not want to sell to a direct rival, but nobody ever told me. Once again, I was in limbo. That was when Pellegrini summoned me to his office again. He was a bit more blunt this time. 'What are you doing? You know you have to leave, right?' he said. By that stage, he'd already found my replacement, Bacary Sagna, who had spent years at Arsenal and had exactly the sort of profile that City needed. That meant I would not only not be in the first team, I wouldn't even be in the squad. I wouldn't even be there to tick a box. I'd be out in the cold, unregistered, unable to play. I couldn't help thinking that there was some small possibility that I'd cocked this up a bit. I had a week, maybe less, to find someone willing to pay me to play football.

The offer of salvation came from somewhere completely unexpected, and only partly because I didn't actually know where it was. My agent had a business partner, a guy called

Dan Wilson, who happened to know a sporting director called Eduardo Macià. Eduardo had been sporting director at Liverpool a few years earlier, when Rafa Benítez was in charge. They'd thought about signing me then, and he obviously hadn't forgotten the powerful impression the young Micah Richards made. He was in Italy now, working for Fiorentina, and he'd got in touch with Dan to ask if I might be interested in joining them on loan.

As a player, the first thing you do when a team is interested in signing you is work out where exactly the team is based. I'd heard of Fiorentina, of course. Anyone who loves football has heard of Fiorentina. The very word conjures up images of Gabriel Batistuta and Rui Costa. They're not high-definition images, obviously, they're quite grainy images, because the club's glory days were in the 1990s, but still: Fiorentina's name carries a bit of weight. That didn't mean I knew where it was, though. I had to go on Wikipedia to find that out. Fiorentina, apparently, is in Florence. OK, I thought, I could deal with Florence. Tick.

The second thing you do, since you've got Wikipedia open, is have a little flick through who's in the team. I knew that Fiorentina used to be a major power, but my immediate thought was that they weren't especially good these days. Batistuta and Rui Costa were a long time ago, after all. Who'd replaced them? I was quite pleased by the answer. Giuseppe Rossi, the Italy striker? Tick. Mario Gómez, the German international? Tick. You're looking for players that you have heard of, players who make you think that the level might be OK.

Even better, though, is finding a couple of players who you know. There was my old friend Stefan Savić, the Manchester City legend. He was at Fiorentina now, was he? That's good. We weren't especially close in his time in England – he was one of the Balkan Boys, with Aleksandar Kolarov and Edin Džeko – but I remembered him as a nice guy, and in those moments, you latch on to anyone you can and do not let go. I texted him and asked him what it was like. He said he loved it. Then I noticed Marcos Alonso, too. He'd played at Bolton for a year, and we had a mutual friend in Daniel Sturridge. That encouraged me: between him and Savić, I knew that there would be at least a couple of people who spoke English. That was enough for me. Let's give this a go, I thought.

That spirit of adventure lasted for about 24 hours. I was in Florence the next morning: I'd taken a train down to London as soon as I'd finished reading the squad list, and then got a flight out from City airport at the crack of dawn. We're not talking a private jet here. There was no helicopter dispatched to collect me. That's the image of the transfer window, and it's the image that football likes to project, but most deals aren't quite that glamorous. I was on a budget flight. I had 10 kilograms of carry-on luggage. We didn't even pay extra to put anything in the hold. We couldn't even upgrade to premium economy.

I was in Italy by about 10 a.m. The news had leaked out enough for there to be a few cameras at the airport. It was quite a big deal for an Italian team to be taking a player from the reigning Premier League champions, even if the player in question had two knees that were of questionable use and was coming in on a budget airline. The club had sent someone to meet us, guide us through the chaos at the airport, and take us to a hotel in the middle of town, where I'd wait until they were ready to do my medical.

It was in the hotel that everything hit me. The outskirts of Florence, it's fair to say, are not quite as pretty as the centre. The drive in from the airport isn't all that inspiring. The hotel wasn't great, either. It was fine, but they hadn't exactly pulled out all the stops. That is when all of the excitement and the adrenaline starts to fade away, and you realise what's happening, the scale of what you're doing. You're sitting in a mid-range hotel in a city you don't know, in a place where you don't understand the language, waiting to find out if you are fit enough to play for a team that you didn't even know was based here until you looked it up. It's hard not to think, at a time like that, that maybe you should have signed the contract at Manchester City. Being a mascot isn't so bad.

Once everything is in motion, though, you're swept along by it. There was a medical to complete, so we went to do it. The club knew about the problems with my knee, obviously, but after a scan they decided that because Serie A is a little slower than the Premier League, I'd be able to cope. They were far more worried about a problem in my hip. That came as a bit of a surprise to me, because I didn't know I had a problem in my hip.

It must have been some sort of arthritis or irregular bone structure: something serious enough to set off an alarm, anyway. While they were going through it, I was installed at the training ground to wait. I noticed there was only one pitch; it wasn't quite as grand as City Football Academy, the state-of-the-art facility City had moved into, right in the shadow of the Etihad. Again, I started to worry. I was way out of my comfort zone here. Why was I moving to Italy? I didn't want to move to Italy.

And then there was another hitch. For some reason, the paperwork wasn't coming through, the bits that needed to be signed and sealed before the move could take place. After a while, it became clear the problem wasn't the medical: the doctors had decided the hip problem I didn't know I had could be managed. It was, it turned out, to do with the deal itself. All of a sudden, City had decided they didn't want to loan me out for free. Fiorentina, they'd figured out, needed someone who could play as a right-back, a wing-back and a central defender: they needed someone with my exact profile. That meant City could try and get a fee for the deal. They wanted a few hundred thousand pounds, and Fiorentina obviously tried to haggle them down. I'd been there all day by this stage and was just sitting around, twiddling my thumbs. I was trying to look calm and collected, but deep down I was stressed. Part of me was worried it was all going to fall through, and I'd have to go home with my tail between my legs. Another part of me was hoping that it would fall through, and that I'd get to go home, no matter where my tail might be.

Some time that night, the two clubs managed to come to an agreement on the fee. I was told that the paperwork had come through. The deal had been completed. I was now, for a year, a Fiorentina player. At long last, just as I had always suspected, me and Gabriel Batistuta had something in common.

The plan, originally, had been for me to come out for a day and then fly home to collect my things. I'd travelled with just the bare necessities: a couple of pairs of underwear, no more than that. I didn't even have a bottle of ketchup on me. But it turned out the club had changed their minds. It was the international break, and the manager, Vincenzo Montella, wanted to have a look at me. I was told I had to stay out for a couple of days longer, and report for training the next morning.

Those next few days were tough. The club did all they could to make me feel comfortable. Eduardo Macià asked his assistant, a Spanish woman who spoke perfect English, to help me settle in. She was unbelievable, an example of exactly what a player liaison officer should be. She could see I was anxious, and she spent all of her time trying to make me feel more comfortable.

Fiorentina's owners, at the time, ran the fashion brand Hogan: they told me I could go and add a couple of things to my wardrobe for free at one of their shops in the city. But that didn't make up for the unease I felt at training. All of the big stars, all of the names I'd recognised, were off on international duty. I was left with the B team, the ones who didn't play for their countries. The standard was – and I'll be nice about this – not quite what I was used to. I didn't recognise any of their players. Nobody seemed to speak English. I didn't really understand what was going on. One day, we travelled north to the Swiss border to play a friendly. I'd gone, in less than a month, from looking forward to another season on the immaculate pitches of the Premier League to playing in some field near Switzerland with a load of people I didn't know. When the time came to go back to England, to pack up my life and head out to Italy permanently, I wasn't exactly enthusiastic. It was just me, on my own. My partner was staying in England. I didn't know anybody. I didn't have anywhere to live. Me and my big mouth.

The next time I turned up for training, though, everything was different. The big boys had come back. Gómez was there. Rossi was there. Savić was there. Marko Marin, who'd played for Chelsea, was there. Milan Badelj, a Croatian international, was there. All of a sudden, the level was unbelievable. That first training session was class. But what really made the difference was what happened afterwards.

For the first time, there were people I could communicate with. I knew Alonso and Savić would speak English, but so did Gómez and Marin and Badelj. They asked me where I was staying. When I gave them the name of the hotel – and remember, this is just a normal hotel, it's not some sort of rat-infested dive – they laughed. That was just where the club put the players while they were doing their medicals, they said. Nobody expected you to live there. That afternoon, they said, they'd show me what playing for Fiorentina was about.

All five of us headed into the city, straight to Mario Gómez's apartment. Things have changed a little bit in England in the last few years – quite a few Manchester City players now live in apartments in the city centre, as does Pep Guardiola – but for the most part, Premier League players tend to live outside cities. That's where you can get a house with plenty of space and, most importantly, a little bit of privacy. In Italy, it's the opposite. The whole squad lived right in the middle of Florence. But none of them had a place quite as nice as Mario Gómez.

It was a penthouse, the entire top floor of a grand old building just round the corner from Piazza degli Strozzi. From his living room, he had a view right across the city, all of the domes and cupolas, the light reflecting off the red-tiled roofs. It was incredible. As soon as I saw it, I made a little note that I'd be looking for a penthouse of my own. I couldn't be letting Mario Gómez have the best flat.

Then we went out for a little tour. Gómez, Alonso, Marin and Badelj showed me all of the sights of Florence – the churches and the piazzas and the bridges over the Arno – and as they did so they pointed out the places that meant the most to them. Fuor d'Acqua, a restaurant serving the best seafood you'll ever eat. Barolo, the typical Italian where they would make sure you had the best evening possible. Pinchiorri, where the food was unbelievable. Golden View, just down the river from the Ponte Vecchio, a place so good that I still go and see them whenever I can, and a place out in the hills, a little bit of a drive, where the meat was the best you could taste.

As soon as we stopped to eat, I could tell they weren't joking. We sat in the sunshine, eating pasta, enjoying a glass of wine, watching the city go by. Then the main course would come. Maybe another glass of wine. I'd spent my entire career as a professional footballer basically going to Nando's. This was another level. From that point on, I was absolutely certain that moving to Florence was the best decision I ever made.

Within a couple of weeks, I'd found somewhere to live. The club had an employee, Cynthia, who helped players find homes. I'd told her that really I'd quite like to live in Mario Gómez's house, was there any way she could boot him out for me, but she went one better. The first place she showed me belonged to Luca Toni, the World Cup-winning Italy striker who had spent a few years at Fiorentina. It was right by the Ponte Vecchio, right in the heart of the city, and it had just been refurbished. I was in love with it as soon as I walked in. This doesn't say a great deal for how sensible I was, but I told her I'd take it before she'd even mentioned a price.

My afternoons, then, followed the pattern Gómez, Alonso and the others had set on that first day. We'd head into the city straight from training. We'd go out for lunch, have a little walk in the sunshine, then join up again for dinner. The food was incredible. Now I understood why so many Italian managers seemed to have such a problem with ketchup. They don't need ketchup. How often, when you go to Italy, do you find yourself sitting in a restaurant, thinking this beautifully prepared dish just needs a big dollop of red on the side? Maybe that is what Roberto Mancini and Fabio Capello couldn't understand. Why did we insist on using tomato sauce, when we could just season our food properly in the first place?

It was more than the food, though. The standard of living was different to anything I'd ever experienced. Part of it is the weather, of course – nobody wants to linger over a glass of wine in the pouring rain – but it felt to me like we weren't really living in England. We were surviving. In Italy, they take their time to enjoy life. Even as a player, when you're meant to concentrate on nothing but football, it's assumed that your quality of life is just as important as the game. It opened my mind.

I'd never really had the ambition to live abroad; it had never seemed particularly possible growing up as a kid in Chapeltown. Now, I was on this adventure, and I loved every second of it. I had a little crew of mates, the English speakers, and it grew by one in January, when Fiorentina brought another player in on loan.

Mohamed Salah had been a bit of a star at Basel, but he'd struggled to get much game time after signing for Chelsea a couple of years before. As soon as he arrived in Florence, though, you could see he was different to everyone else. In his first training session, he picked the ball up and danced straight past about five players, before dinking the ball over the goalkeeper. When you see someone do something like that, you know straightaway. He's going to be a proper player. In fact, you see it even more clearly as a defender. You can tell when someone takes you on. If you can't get close to them, if there's nothing you can do to stop them, you can be pretty sure they're special. And Salah was very special.

Giuseppe Rossi was, in theory, the big star at Fiorentina, but he'd always struggled with injuries. Gómez was the experienced German international, too, another big name, but for some reason he couldn't quite take his chances in

Italy. He was a brilliant finisher, but he seemed to need a handful before he could actually score. Salah, on the other hand, wasn't messing about. He showed flashes of what he could do in his first few appearances, but it was a goal against Juventus – the team that Fiorentina fans hate more than anyone else – in the Coppa Italia that made him a star. He picked the ball up deep inside his own half and drove at the Juventus defence, going past three or four players before producing an unstoppable shot back across the goalkeeper. He got a second later on, and we won the game and the tie.

From that point on, Salah was the king, and people treated him as such. He spoke good English from his time at Chelsea, so he'd started to hang around with us when he first came to Florence. He lived not too far from me, so quite a lot of the time it would just be me and him, or me, him and Marcos Alonso, sitting and having a coffee some-where in the city, watching the world go by. He was one of the nicest, most humble people I'd ever met, and I've had a soft spot for him ever since. But his talent meant that he couldn't do that for long. After a while, the fans loved him so much that there would be people camped outside his house most of the time; he definitely couldn't walk the streets like the rest of us. He'd be mobbed. After a while, he'd go home after training. He was a quiet guy anyway, but when you're that good, and that adored, you don't really have much of a choice.

I didn't make quite as much of an impression on the pitch – you'll be surprised to learn that I struggled a bit with injuries – but I did well enough for the club to offer to extend my contract. My deal at City was going to expire on 1 July, and Fiorentina made a bid to sign me up permanently. It was a really difficult choice. I loved my life in Florence. I even learned a bit of Italian. 'Prego' means you're welcome, for example. Except when it means something else. Other black players have experienced racism either on the pitch or away from it in Italy, and it is an issue that the country's football authorities have often handled dreadfully, but I always felt welcome. I felt settled enough, anyway, that I started to look at flats to buy.

When the contract offer came, though, I wasn't quite sure. I couldn't work out if the club wanted to sign me as a bit of a smart piece of business – there's value in having an English player, because there's always a decent chance an English club will come and sign them, thanks to the quota – rather than because they wanted me to play for them. I was worried that I'd find myself out of the team again pretty quickly after signing. Then there was the manager: I wasn't sure if I'd completely earned Vincenzo Montella's trust. I didn't know if he wanted me, or if the club did.

That wasn't the only thing that played on my mind. As a kid, even before you're in an academy, you dream of playing in the Premier League. You might support a team, but whoever it is, it's being a Premier League player that feels like the ultimate ambition. That is where you prove yourself. That is where you show that you're good enough. That's the ultimate test.

No matter how happy I was in Florence, there was part of me that worried that moving away from England permanently was proof that I'd failed that test. Maybe not in the early part of my career, but at the peak of it, at the age of 27. Signing for Fiorentina would have been me accepting that I was no longer as good as I used to be, that I couldn't cut it anymore, that I wasn't in the biggest league in the world. I couldn't shake that idea. So when Aston Villa came in for me, I decided to turn down Fiorentina's offer and accept Tim Sherwood's. It's not that living in Birmingham held more appeal than waking up every morning to a view of the Ponte Vecchio. It was that anything less than the Premier League, in some way, felt like failure.

I think that's the way a lot of players see it, and I wish I could tell them how wrong they are. One of the most welcome developments in the last few years is seeing young English kids having the nerve to go out and play in Germany or, more rarely, Italy or France or Spain. Just getting that life experience, coming out of your comfort zone, challenging yourself, is something incredibly courageous. I'd encourage anyone who has the chance to do it to go for it.

There is part of me, definitely, that wishes that I'd stayed for longer. My time at Villa, as an overwhelming majority of Villa fans will tell you, was not an especially happy one. For them, mainly. This won't get much sympathy, but it even cost me my chance to have my own place in Italy: relegation at the end of my first season there meant that I had to revise my budget for a little apartment, and I never ended up buying one.

If things had been different – if I'd been able to speak just a little more Italian, if I'd been able to find a decent barber for my hair, if I'd not been worried about saying goodbye to the Premier League – then I'd be writing this from my penthouse overlooking the Arno, the sun setting over the red-tiled roofs, a glass of wine waiting for me on Piazza degli Strozzi, thinking how glad I was to be in Florence, the best place I have ever been, and how happy I was to have made what I thought, at the time, was the biggest mistake of my career.

14
THE END

John Terry's call was exactly what I'd been waiting for. I hadn't kicked a ball for two years. Not properly, anyway. Not in a game. My last appearance for Aston Villa had been in October 2016. I'd come off after an hour then, pretending I had cramp but really worried about the feeling in my knee: I could feel it starting to swell up. Since then, I seemed to have been bouncing from one injury to another. Even when I was fit, I'd not been able to do anything but train. That had been with the first team, at the start. But after a while, I couldn't even do that. I was sent to train with the reserves, the kids, instead. I was stuck.

As soon as JT's name flashed up on my phone, I thought that was about to change. Villa had just appointed Dean Smith as manager. Terry, who I'd known since our days with England together, had been installed as his assistant. The gaffer wanted to see me, he said. It was music to my ears. He was going to offer me a fresh start. All the problems of the last couple of years would be water under the bridge. He'd give me the opportunity to prove myself, to win my place back. I was only 30. I had another couple of years in me, at least. In the Championship, maybe more. Dean Smith was going to offer me the chance to feel like a footballer again.

Or not, as it turned out. I always liked managers who were honest with me, and Dean was completely honest. He didn't try and lead me on. He didn't shirk the difficult conversation. He told me that the way I was moving didn't look right to him. There was something wrong with my knee: he could see it in the way I ran and, most of all, in the way I was slowing down when I had the ball at my feet. I was taking too long to control the ball. It was as though I was very carefully positioning myself before playing a pass just so my knee didn't go. In the process, I was slowing the team down. He wanted to play with a bit of zip. He needed everything to be quick, sharp, instant. I was too ponderous. I couldn't play football the way he wanted to play football. There would, he told me, be no place for me in his Aston Villa team.

I've always liked to feel like I'm real with myself. I can be honest about my shortcomings. I know what I'm good at and what I'm not. During my career, I knew when I'd played well and when I hadn't. I'm not delusional. But as he said it, I didn't really understand. I felt I was playing pretty well in training. I thought I was doing fine. Afterwards, I went to check with the other players. I asked them how they thought I'd been playing. They assured me I was fine, doing well, not a problem. Of course you don't know if they're saying that because they genuinely mean it, or because they don't want to hurt your feelings. Deep down, I was aware that it didn't matter. That conversation with Dean Smith was the end of my career. I knew it. I just didn't want to admit that I knew it, not right away.

As a young player, you can tell when one of your opponents – or even one of your teammates – is coming to the end. For defenders and for forwards, the pace is always the first thing to go. They don't have that explosive burst anymore. For midfielders, it's a bit different. It's their ability to get round the pitch. They can't cover as much ground, and they certainly can't cover it all that quickly.

There are things you can do to compensate for it, early on. In the days when a lot of English football was long ball, a defender could get by just on their ability to read the game. All they had to do was head the ball and kick the ball, head the ball and kick the ball. They didn't have to move. Nobody was asking them to bring the ball out of defence. Nobody was expecting a full-back to be on the overlap. Nobody insisted you had to play in the half-spaces. They hadn't even invented half-spaces back then.

Strikers, too, could survive through sheer physical strength, mixed in with a little bit of street-smarts. A big unit of a forward might, by the time they were 32 or 33, find that the very best teams don't fancy them anymore, but they'd get a move to a smaller club just on their reputation. It wouldn't matter that they'd scored four goals in three years; managers would know that they could find a use for them. All you needed in a forward was someone who protects the ball. You needed a hold-up merchant, a human equivalent of a wall. A striker didn't need to be sprinting all over the shop. They didn't have to learn their pressing triggers. They just had to stand there and be tall.

For players who relied more on their pace, they would have to change the way they played a little more drastically. When Michael Owen scored that winning goal in the Manchester derby – the one that was definitely Shaun Wright-Phillips's fault, if you remember – he was a long way past his best. It wasn't just that he couldn't run, it was that he was scared to run. He didn't want to open up because he was afraid his hamstring might go at any moment. I've been there, and I know what it looks like. You're worried that the next injury is the last, so you do anything you can to prevent it from happening. You adapt the way you play to fit what your body will allow you to do, or what you feel your body will allow you to do. Owen still had his movement. He hadn't lost any of that. But he knew that he couldn't beat you for pace anymore. At his best, if he had the run on a central defender, they wouldn't stand a chance. By the time I played against him, he knew that if he tried to get in behind me, I'd eat him for breakfast. So he started to drop off instead. He'd let me win the first header, and then see if he could work off the second ball.

There comes a point, though, where a player can't adapt any longer. There aren't any more changes to make. You still know what you want to do, because you've spent your whole life doing it, but your body just won't let you. It looks from the outside like your decision-making ability has gone, as though you've lost your head, but it's not that. You know exactly what you need to do in any given situation. It just isn't physically possible anymore. That's the time to call it a day, to ride off into the sunset.

It's much easier to see it in other people than it is yourself, though. Looking back, my career was declining from the time I was 23 or 24. That was my peak. I did not see it at the time. It didn't feel like I was on the slide, because it happened in stages, gradually, over the course of a few years, and because I didn't want to admit it. I was in denial.

My best season, under Roberto Mancini, came in the year City won the title for the first time. That was when I was at my absolute best. It was the year after that the injuries really started to kick in. There was an ankle problem that I picked up during the Olympics, and then my first major knee injury in a game against Swansea City. I was out for four months, and I came back looking just as good as ever. I remember the reaction to my first few appearances being really positive: Micah Richards is back, he's overcome his injury problems, he's just the same as before. I was still young. All players miss a few months through injury every now and again. It's just something that happens. I should have had another decade or so ahead of me. By the end of my career, those four months would have been nothing but a blip.

But something changed after that. City hadn't really missed me. On the pitch, anyway. I'm sure they were all devastated that I wasn't around the changing room for a bit. Who would have masterminded the plots to break into Vincent Kompany's locker without me? Pablo Zabaleta had come in and played brilliantly. He was the first-choice right-back now. On some level, I knew from that moment that my career at the very highest level – as a starter for a team trying to win titles, a regular in the Champions League, one of the best full-backs in the world – was done. I wasn't in control of my own destiny anymore. My injury record wasn't good enough that another top team would come in for me, and even if they had, I'm not sure I'd have wanted to go. I'd come through at City. I loved City. I loved Manchester. I didn't really want to play anywhere else. No, the only way for me to get back to being a Champions League level player, really, was for Pablo to get injured. If he was out for an extended period of time, then I'd get chance to stake my claim again. If not, then all I would ever be at City was a squad player, and if I wasn't at City, I wouldn't be at the top level.

Within two years, that's exactly where I found myself. It was when I was on loan at Fiorentina that I realised I'd fallen a stage further. I started really well in Italy. I got an assist in my first game. I don't know whether it was the slightly slower pace of the league, or whether it was something about the sunshine and the long lunches and living right by the Ponte Vecchio, but it felt to me like I was back. It was a new lease of life. Maybe we weren't in the Champions League, but it was still top-class football, it was still Serie A, still the Europa League.

That, it turned out, was the problem. Italian football believes in what is known as active recovery. Even if you've played on the Saturday or the Sunday, you'll be out jogging on the Monday. I knew my body by that stage, though, and my body likes a massage. I need at least two days of rest before I'm ready to start building up again. That's how long it takes for the power to come back. It meant that, instead of recuperating after my first start in Serie A – against Genoa – I was running within 48 hours, ahead of a Europa League game on the Thursday.

I knew that was a risk. I'm amazed, now, to see the levels that teams like Manchester City and Liverpool can reach and sustain over three games in a week. They never seem to drop off. They don't seem to get fatigued, or to worry about picking up injuries. Even in my mid-twenties, I couldn't do that. I just wasn't built that way. I couldn't deal with the demands of three games in the space of seven days. My body wouldn't recover in time. Sometimes, managers will make allowances for players who need that extra rest. Towards the end of his career at Spurs, Ledley King famously barely trained at all. He'd go in and have a swim, the only exercise that his knees could take, and then play at the weekend anyway. The club knew he'd be able to perform even without training, and that asking him to do any more would just make his injuries worse.

For most of us, though, it's a difficult conversation to have. I couldn't have gone in and seen Vincenzo Montella, my manager in Florence, and explained to him that actually I didn't really fancy playing in the middle of the week, I'd be better having a bit of time off, and not just because my Italian wasn't quite up to it. 'Signor Montella, uno, per favore' wouldn't have made a vast amount of sense to him, really, and that was all I had up my sleeve. Besides, the club was paying my full contract. You can't have someone who's costing you £90,000 a week coming into your office and saying they're not really up for working anti-social hours.

Sure enough, four days after playing against Genoa, I started in the Europa League game and came off within 20 minutes or so with a hamstring injury. I knew, then, that I couldn't really sustain European football any longer. Not because I wasn't good enough, but because my body wouldn't tolerate anything more than one game a week. I could give you one good game a week. But any more than that and I was asking for trouble.

That influenced my decision to come back to England. One of the major factors in signing for Aston Villa, as well as Tim Sherwood's tough love, was the fact that they weren't in Europe. There might be a couple of games in the Carabao Cup, and the odd busy week in the Premier League, but I could be rotated for those. I'd be playing once a week. I thought that would enable me to play to my best within the limits of what I could do, and prolong my career in the process. It was perfect.

Under Sherwood it worked, too. I was made captain for my first game, and I was flying. I didn't pick up a single injury. He made sure that he didn't ask too much of me, physically. Sometimes, in fact, he probably asked too little. I was back living in Manchester at the time and, one week, before a game at Anfield, he told me that I didn't need to worry about coming into training on the Friday. I was his captain, he trusted me. He felt that it would be better for me to rest and relax at home than have to spend hours in the car. As it turned out, that wasn't quite right. I found that, without anything in my legs, I felt really lethargic

during the game. I needed something the day before playing, just to get me in rhythm. I just didn't need very much.

It was when Tim left that things took a turn for the
worse. Rémi Garde and his staff weren't interested in
tailoring training to take all of the players' physical needs
into account. When the first thing they made us do was
that assault course, I knew it wasn't just me suffering. My
back was screaming and my hamstrings were burning and
I could feel my knee swelling up, but there were other
players, too, nursing injuries that they'd picked up during
the course of the season who were just having their problems made worse. The difference might be that most of
them recovered from it. I couldn't. From that point on, all
I could do was manage.

Everyone has a different tolerance for injuries. Some
players are warriors. They'll play through anything short
of a fully detached limb. Others need to feel exactly right
to have the confidence in their body that you need to go
out and perform. If they have a niggle, it will play on their
mind. But as a rule, players will do anything to play.
They'll take an injection or fill themselves with painkillers
or they'll just not tell the doctor that they're in pain.
Everything is always left to the last minute. You might see
a player pick up an injury in a game and assume that
they'll be absent for at least a couple of weeks, but then it
will emerge by the Wednesday that they're ready to go
again. They'll have a scan. They'll let the swelling go
down. They'll get fixed up as best as possible and, if they
feel they can, they'll play. They know that missing one
game might mean they lose their place for the rest of the

season. They might fall down the pecking order. They might end up being sold. One game can make a massive difference.

I was the same. I'd sneak into Bodymoor Heath, Villa's training ground, at 7 a.m. every day. Before any of the players or the coaching staff had arrived, I'd go for a swim just to get my muscles warm. I'd do all of my pre-activation, the warm-up exercises to reduce the risk of injury. I'd take three 75-milligram Voltarol tablets in one go. Then, when I'd already been there for hours, everyone else would pitch up and we'd go and train. Afterwards, I'd wrap my knee in ice. I'd take another three Voltarol to try to keep the swelling down. After a while, when that was no longer enough, I took more extreme measures. A doctor would come to my flat in Birmingham, take out a big syringe, and drain the fluid from my knee. I'd see it coming out: 40 millilitres, 50 millilitres, 60, 70. All this disgusting yellow goo being drawn out of my leg. Not so I could play a game, just so I could train. He told me, time and again, that I was messing with my health, that I shouldn't be doing it to my body, that all of that liquid was a message from my knee, that it wasn't worth it. I'd respond that everything we were doing was perfectly legal, that it was my body, that this is what I needed to do. I had a couple of years left on my contract and I was smart enough to know that I wouldn't get another one. Nobody in their right mind would sign me once they'd seen the state my knee was in. I needed to get to the end of this contract, so let's just do whatever we can to make sure I'm available. Just get me through the next couple of years.

I can see now the impossible position I was putting him in. It wasn't fair of me. We still get on well, but I feel incredibly guilty about it. It's fine to have your knee drained of fluid every now and again. Maybe once a year, something like that. I was making him do it every six to eight weeks, and all because I had an idea in my head of what I needed to be doing, of what I ought to be doing. I was putting him, and me, through all of that just because I couldn't quite accept what should really have been obvious as soon as the syringe went in: that my body wouldn't let me play football anymore. I'd made the final step. I'd accepted that I couldn't be a Champions League player. I'd accepted that I couldn't physically deal with European football. Now I needed to accept that football as a whole was too much. I had known that it would come at some point, but I wasn't prepared for it to come so soon. I was only 30, and it was over.

It was the doctor, eventually, who got through to me. I was raging for a week after my conversation with Dean Smith. I thought it was just another excuse, a way of blaming me for the fact that I wasn't in their plans. The doctor, though, told me that if I kept on torturing my body, draining the fluid from my knee just so I could train, then I wouldn't be able to run around with my kids and my grandkids. He was right, too. Now, after a day sitting down in a studio, my knee seizes up. I find myself limping when I get up. I might put an extra bit of sauce on there, style it out a little bit, but it's the cumulative effect of all the injuries. It would have been far worse if he'd not finally got in my head. He snapped me out of it. It's a cliché but I realised that I had to think about what came after football, too. The time had come to call it a day.

That's easier said than done. Some players retire with a bit of grace: a nice presentation on the pitch, a farewell video, lots of tributes on social media. Not me. I hadn't played for two years at that point, and Dean Smith wasn't exactly the first manager to make it clear that he didn't really have any use for me, but for some reason Villa had refused to sell me.

They'd had offers. The most serious interest came the year we were relegated. West Ham, who had tried to sign me from Fiorentina, came back. They wanted to sign me on loan for a season, with the option of buying me at the end of it. It was an appealing idea. Not just because they were in the Premier League, but because they were in the Premier League and not in Europe. They would play one game a week. The Championship, on the other hand, was relentless, with games every three days. I knew I couldn't manage that. Villa knew I couldn't manage that. But West Ham promised they would take care of my knee, not push me too hard, allow me the time to recover that would enable me to play for a few more years.

Villa, though, said no. They saw me as an asset and they wanted a fee for me. My then agent and good friend, James Black, tried to explain to them that this was an easy way to get me off the wage bill. He told them that my knee meant I wouldn't be able to play regularly for them. He pointed out that they would get a fee for me if West Ham took up the option. They still wouldn't budge.

It got so bad, so frustrating, that I drove to Villa Park

on transfer deadline day to plead my case with the club. James and I decided it would be more powerful if, instead of getting my agent to do my dirty work, I went to see Keith Wyness, the chief executive, personally. I pitched up in his office, knowing full well that if he finally relented then I would have time to go down to London and do my medical at West Ham. I told him that I wouldn't be able to give the club what it needed. I asked him to let me leave. I made all the same arguments that James had made. He did not listen. The manager, he told me, would use me in whatever way was best for the club. There would be no move. We had to call West Ham and tell them the deal was a no go.

That was not the last offer for my services that Villa refused. Sunderland came back in for me, too, and a few months later I had the chance to move abroad again. Jason Kreis, a former Under-23 coach at Manchester City, had taken a job in Major League Soccer with Orlando, and he'd asked if I'd be interested in going over there. Florida is very similar to Birmingham, so that would have worked perfectly. I don't know if I'd have passed a medical, but it didn't matter. Villa kept asking for a fee. They wanted someone to pay them money for a player they clearly didn't want. Even Sunderland weren't going to do that.

I couldn't quite tell you why they didn't just want me out of the door. The kind version is that they knew I was important in the dressing room, that even if they weren't losing anything in terms of the team, that I still had a value to them as part of the squad. That is something that I'm genuinely proud of: no matter how bad things got, no matter how tense it was between me and the club, my professionalism never dropped. Having an unhappy senior player can be dangerous for a team: what had happened between Rémi Garde and Gabby Agbonlahor proved that. But I was never anything less than positive. I was helpful. Cheery, even. Maybe Villa recognised that.

Or maybe they didn't. Maybe they wanted a return on what they'd paid me. Maybe they wanted a scapegoat. There were definitely times when I made myself an easy target. In 2018, I was on holiday in Ibiza when a guy approached me. He was very friendly, very pleasant, Brummie accent. He was a big Villa fan, he said, and he'd just started a hat company. He was wondering if I could do a selfie with him to help promote it. Of course, I said, no problem at all. He told me that the company's logo was a sort of letter Z. Could I just do that with my hands, and then he'd put it up on Instagram? I thought nothing of it. It seemed like quite a good logo for a hat company. He thanked me, and everyone got on with their day.

A few hours later, my phone started blowing up. All of these messages were pouring in. Friends were getting in touch, asking what I'd done. Twitter and Instagram were full of Villa fans abusing me. I had no idea why. It turned out that I wasn't in an impromptu advert for a hat company. The guy wasn't a Villa fan. The 'Z' sign is the hand gesture for Birmingham City's old hooligan firm, the Zulus. He'd tricked me into making it, and now it looked like the player Villa were paying a fortune not to play for them was taking the piss out of the club. I tried to apologise, tried to explain, made it clear that amazingly I don't know a lot about the hand gestures of 1980s hooligan firms. None of it worked. What little sympathy I had from Villa's fans disappeared from then on.

By the time I was ready to accept that my career was over, relations between me and the club were at a bit of a low point. They made an offer to pay up part of my contract. I would probably have accepted that, a year or so before, but I felt they'd put me through so much that I wasn't in the mood to do them a favour. I'd kept my dignity. I'd never gone public with my complaints. I'd never tried to throw anyone under the bus. In return, the club had refused offers to let me go, and somehow the newspapers seemed to have an extremely good idea of the fine detail of my contract. The longer they'd left me to rot, the more it had messed with my head. I wasn't going to accept a low-ball offer to get rid of me now. I'd see out the contract they had agreed with me.

One of the brighter parts of my time at Aston Villa was getting to see a young Jack Grealish flourish. He blew me away the first time I trained with him. I hadn't previously seen a player dribble with his quality nor dance round players so easily, without needing a trick. Alongside Daniel Sturridge and Michael Johnson, he was in the best trio of youngsters I ever played with.

There were similarities between the two of us – after all, a decade before, I had been the teenage star making the jump from the academy to play for the first team. At the time, I spoke in the media about how Jack had to quickly learn from his mistakes off the pitch and concentrate on giving 100 per cent when he was on it. How quickly you can become a 'dad' in the dressing room.

By the time my contract ended at Aston Villa, Jack was well on his way to becoming the player Manchester City would go on to pay £100 million for in the summer of 2021. Since I started working in the media, colleagues have often joked that I'm the leader of the Jack Grealish fan club. I always will be. We're good friends and I believe he's still got a lot of success ahead of him.

Those final few months were some of the darkest of my life. Dean Smith, as ever, had been good with me. He'd asked me what I wanted to do. I wouldn't be training with the first team. I didn't have any intention of training with the reserves, either. They had their own schedule, based around their games, and it seemed a bit pointless to drive down every day for certain times when I knew I wouldn't be playing for them. I told him that I wouldn't be sneaking in and out of the training ground, either going to the gym before the first team had arrived or after they'd left. I wasn't a naughty schoolboy being kept in detention. Instead, we came to an uneasy – but deep down incredibly strange – truce. I'd moved back from Manchester to Harrogate by that stage. Three times a week, I'd make the drive down to Birmingham. I'd go into the training ground. I'd have a bit of banter with the lads. I'd do some stuff in the gym. Then I'd go home again. I was going to spend nine months as the world's highest-paid cheerleader.

I was good at it, too. I'll allow myself a little pat on the back. I did nothing but spread positive vibes whenever I was with the team. I didn't badmouth the manager. I didn't try and create problems for anyone. I was my usual charming self. The players would ask me what I was doing with my day, and I'd respond with a big smile and a bit of a laugh and tell them that I might stay down for the night, head into London, do a bit of shopping, get a bite to eat. I portrayed myself as a gentleman of leisure, and very happy about it, too. I think my presence that year helped. It certainly didn't make anyone's life difficult. I lightened the mood. I helped keep morale up. It was good for them to have me around, I think.

It was different at home. I knew how muggy it was going in not to play, not to train, but just to mess about in the gym and be the butt of a joke. It was hard enough knowing that my career was over. It's something that all players struggle to understand and to accept. You don't know how to do anything else. It's been your life since you were a teenager. It's been your dream since you were a kid. And now it's done, and you have to figure out what will come next, how you'll fill your days. Being a footballer isn't just a very privileged and occasionally ridiculous job. It's also an identity. It is who you are. When it comes to an end, you lose more than your income. I had no idea how to deal with it.

That was bad enough, but for it to end as it did was far, far worse. In the space of six years I'd gone from being a Premier League champion, a Champions League player, an England international, into being the sort of person who turns up at the training ground and isn't even allowed to train with the kids. I wasn't going out in a blaze of glory. My career was fizzling out into nothing.

I have relatives who have struggled with their mental health. It is something, now, that I think about a lot, having seen what they have been through. Maybe it is harder to recognise the symptoms in yourself. Maybe you don't notice the small changes, the ones that happen over weeks and months. Maybe you don't spot when you have stopped smiling, or when nothing seems to lift the clouds, or when you find it hard to be motivated to do anything.

Looking back, now, I wonder if I was suffering from depression in those last couple of years at Aston Villa. I was smiling and joking for my teammates, acting as though I was having the time of my life, but the only place I really wanted to be was at my mum's house, with the people who knew me best, with the people who really cared about me, the people who had my back. Nobody did that more than my friend Maj Khadim, who would often remind me of all the good things I had in my life and helped me to concentrate on reasons to be thankful.

Most players who mention their mental health are shouted down. They're told that they have nothing to worry about: how can you be struggling when you're rich? And that's true, you know. I never had to worry that I couldn't provide for people. It wasn't just my immediate family I had to support, it was aunts and uncles and cousins and friends, but I had been sensible. I could look after them. That was a relief.

But mental health isn't related to money. You can suffer, too, no matter how comfortable you are. I wasn't under financial pressure, but there were all sorts of other strains. I had always seen it as my job to fly the flag, not just for my family but for my community, too. As a young black man, you are not permitted to make mistakes; if you do, all black people are judged. I always felt as though there was a lot more than just me depending on my success. When I started to feel like I was failing, then it felt like I was letting everyone else down, too.

And then there was the question of identity. I was a footballer. It wasn't just my job. It was who I was. But for two years, Villa had not let me be one. They had refused to let me leave. They had denied me the chance to do the thing that always defined me. Now it was all ebbing away, and there was nothing I could do about it. I was powerless.

My mum knew something was wrong. She could tell that I wasn't myself. The person you see on television is the real me: I do try to take the joy from life. That is how I have always been. That is who I am. It wasn't then. That is the lowest I have ever been. Even when my mum asked, I didn't want to talk about it. I didn't know how to tell her, or what to say. I didn't have the words to explain that I wasn't a footballer anymore and didn't know how to deal with it.

15

YOU CAN BLAME BRETT FOR WHAT HAPPENED NEXT

Sometimes, you just take to something completely naturally. This was the case with me and broadcasting. From the very first time I did it, as a wide-eyed 17-year-old, it was obvious that I had a gift. A God-given talent.

I'd only made a couple of starts for Manchester City when I did my first television interview. It was after an FA Cup game at Villa Park, shown live on the BBC. I'd scored a 90th-minute equaliser to take the game to a replay, so I was the player they requested to speak to after the match. I didn't really have time to think about what I was going to say. I had no idea what I was supposed to do. Still out of breath from the game, I was taken straight from the pitch and presented to Garth Crooks, holding a microphone. The light on the camera changed. And all of a sudden, he was asking what I made of it all.

'Ah, it was just great to be out there,' I said. A good start. A solid start. Maybe this wasn't so tough after all. 'Fucking, I just can't believe it. One minute we were one–nil down, and then last minute, we got the goal.'

Now I knew what I'd done as soon as I'd said it. But it had been an honest mistake. It had been very quick. People might not have noticed it. Besides, I was a kid. The viewers would allow me a little bit of leeway. Maybe Garth would just breeze past it, pretend it hadn't happened. He definitely wouldn't draw attention to it.

'Now you're a young kid and we can understand your excitement,' he said. 'But this is going out to a national audience, so be careful what you say.'

Thanks, Garth.

In the last couple of years, I've found more and more current players getting in touch with me to ask about how to get into broadcasting. Once you've retired, it's one of two desirable career options, and if we're all honest it's quite a lot easier than being a manager. They'll pick my brains about what the best route to get into it might be, what to avoid, how to make sure you're a success. They'll see if there's any advice I can give them.

The first thing is always the same: whatever you do, make sure you swear the first time you're live on the BBC. The second is a bit trickier. It's very important, I tell them, to get a head start on everyone else from your generation, so do what you can to pick up so many injuries as a player that you find yourself forced to retire much earlier than all of your Premier League-title-winning teammates.

My playing career was over by the time I was 30. I'd been very careful in investing the money I'd made while times were good, so I knew I'd be OK financially, but I'd never really thought about what I'd actually do once I wasn't playing anymore, how I'd fill my days. I'd got some experience in television without really meaning to do so: I'd been a regular guest on Manchester City's own TV station while I was there, initially because I was seen as a bit of a weak link by the press officers – I was less likely to say no than everyone else – and then because, thanks to all of the injuries I had in my last season, there wasn't much else to do. I'd always tried to be light-hearted and energetic, but I'd not done it with any great plan in mind.

That, combined with me swearing at Garth Crooks, had obviously been enough to attract the attention of the BBC. In my last year at Villa, I had a few requests to do a little bit of punditry work. I was quite a valuable property. Not because of my good looks and charm so much as the fact that there were very few faces who represented the modern Manchester City on television. Most of them were still playing. Only Joleon Lescott had started to do a bit here and there. The more titles they won and the more success they had, the better it was for everyone to have a guest who knew the club, and the people at the club, first-hand. I'd played with a lot of the players storming clear at the top of the Premier League under Pep Guardiola. Better still, I knew what it was like to win a title for Manchester City. That gave me a bit of insight into what was happening, at least in theory.

At first, I said no. It seemed like a recipe for even more criticism from Villa fans: happily taking my wage and then spending every Saturday in the studios at Sky or the BBC, rather than actually playing. The fact that it wasn't my choice wouldn't have mattered a bit. Out of respect for the club, I wanted to wait until I had actually retired. When that happened, though, I didn't feel ready. I was still licking my wounds after the way my career had ended. I wanted to hide myself away. I worried that if I appeared on television pontificating about this and that, people would ask quite what right someone who hadn't been able to get into a Championship team for two years had to have an opinion. I'd gone from being a Premier League champion to being accused of stealing money from a struggling team, and it was embarrassing.

It was a random message on Instagram that changed everything. If you've got tired of seeing my face on *Match of the Day* and Sky and in the newspapers and hearing my voice on the radio over the last few years, you can direct all of your complaints to Brett.

Brett was an Aston Villa fan, in the proper sense of the word. I got to know him a little in the days when I did actually play for Villa, when I had reason to drive out of Villa Park at the weekend. He'd be one of the fans waiting for the players to leave. You start to recognise the faces after a while. It tends to be the same people, most of the time. A lot of them might as well be called 'eBay'. Brett was a bit different. No matter how we'd done, whether we'd won or lost – and to be fair we'd normally lost – Brett would have a kind word. He'd say something complimentary about the performance. Instead of asking for things to be signed, he'd bring things to give to the players. He once gave me a washbag with my name on it, just big enough for a bottle of ketchup. He was in his teens, I think, and he used to come down with his mum. He seemed a good kid.

We weren't in touch or anything, but every so often I'd sort him out with tickets for games, that sort of thing. A little while after I'd retired, he sent me a message on Instagram. I don't know why, but it seemed to knock me into gear. It was as positive and as encouraging as he'd always been. He told me that he knew I'd been through a lot, but that I shouldn't forget how good a player I'd been, and that he was sure that I had a different story to tell to the one that the club had put out. I'd won the Premier League; I shouldn't let the way things had ended affect me.

I don't quite know why he chose to send me that message. He was probably the only Villa fan in the world who didn't think I was a mercenary. But it struck a chord. It occurred to me that he was right: my career hadn't quite gone the way I might have hoped, but maybe that was a blessing. I'd seen the highs and the lows, and I could explain what both felt like. Maybe I did have a story to tell. I decided that I might as well see if anyone wanted to hear it.

Just like football itself, football punditry runs according to a strict hierarchy. At the top of it, you have the pundit heavyweights: Alan Shearer, a legend of the game. Gary Lineker, a former England captain. Roy Keane and Graeme Souness, who won it all. Ian Wright, one of my childhood heroes. Gary Neville, a Manchester United hero. Jamie Redknapp, as insightful as they come. Jamie Carragher, who captained Liverpool when Steven Gerrard was injured. They're the big dogs.

Meeting them can be intimidating. Not just because of what they achieved as players, but because they've become the best in their field after retiring, too. I only ever remember being star-struck twice as a player. Once was with David Beckham, when we played together with England. I don't know what it was about Beckham, but he just looked like he was better than you. Like a human, but improved. You could be wearing exactly the same training gear, and you'd look like you'd got yours out of the bargain bin at Donnay Sports, and he'd look like he was coming off a catwalk. The other was with Patrick Vieira. I'd loved Vieira as a player, so the day he turned up at City I came over all shy. I didn't know what to say to him before our first training session. I knew exactly what to say to him afterwards, though. 'You're horrible.' I've never encountered a dirtier player in my life. He was a lovely man, but there was no situation Patrick Vieira didn't think could be improved by raking his studs down your shin. By the time we got back to the changing room, I was comfortable enough to tell him that playing against him once was enough to turn my love for him into a mixture of fear and hatred. He laughed. I liked Patrick a lot. As long as he was on my team.

Sitting in a room with those players as pundits, though, was daunting. They're all friendly and welcoming and happy to offer a bit of advice, but at the same time, a footballer is always a footballer. They always think like footballers. Just as a squad will reserve judgement on a new signing until they've seen them in a rondo, established pundits will wait to see what you can do. It's not arrogance. They just want to know that you deserve your seat.

That's the level you aspire to reach, but you have to earn it. You have to cut your teeth. No matter how glittering your career, you have to prove you can do it. You have to iron out the mistakes. Being a footballer and talking about being a footballer on television are two very different things. To be good at it, it's not enough just to turn up and be a familiar face. It's not even enough to know football. You get the chance because of all the experiences you've had, but you only get to stay there if you can articulate them properly, make them interesting and entertaining, while coping with all of the demands of live television. There are different cameras to look at. There are people talking in your ear. There are strict time limits on how long you should speak. It isn't quite as easy as it looks. And nobody, really, prepares you for it.

My first appearance in a studio went roughly as badly as my first interview on the BBC, though at least this time I didn't have Garth Crooks there to point out what I'd done wrong. I'd been booked to do *Football Focus*, a bit of a trial run, to see if I enjoyed it, and to see if they thought I could do it. I was on with Dan Walker and Alex Scott. The plan was to start with a little bit of banter. Dan would ask me what I was looking forward to from my first pre-season since retirement, and I'd say something along the lines of not having to run around and the chance to eat a few pies. At no point would I accidentally say 'fuck'.

Just as Dan started the question, I heard the producer say in my ear not to forget to mention the pies. That was the punchline. I had to deliver it just right. But it threw me off my rhythm completely. Dan finished his question. I blurted something out about pre-season pies. I'd messed it up completely. The only thing that saved me was the fact that we'd decided to pre-record the introduction to the show; it wasn't live. I'd get a second go. Nobody ever said anything, but I suspect in the control room they were busy scratching my name out of next week's show. Get Dion Dublin to do it. He's a professional. He knows how to deliver a gag.

For some reason, though, the BBC stuck with me. I worked out a deal with Sky, too, and started working my way up the ladder. It's all a test, in a way, to see if you're ready for the twin peaks of football punditry: *Super Sunday* and *Match of the Day*. They're the big ones. You don't get either of those without someone up there liking you. Not God, necessarily, just some sort of executive producer, but in this context those two forces are equally powerful.

Match of the Day is the hardest gig in television, no question. It's a long day, for a start. *Football Focus* is a breeze by comparison: you turn up at 10.30 a.m., slap a bit of make-up on, do an hour, and then you're finished. You might stick around to do *Final Score*, but either way, you're on the way home by 6 p.m. Those are the sorts of working hours a footballer can understand. *Match of the Day*, on the other hand, is a marathon.

The first time I was invited to do it, I was really hoping it would be me and Ian Wright. I'd played with Shaun and Bradley Wright-Phillips, so we had something in common; besides, I'd always thought of him as a sort of friendly uncle. There was the slight awkwardness of knowing that I'd had a go at him on Twitter at some point after he criticised one of my performances, but I thought having him there might put me at my ease. No such luck. It was me, Shearer, the most thorough man in football, and Gary Lineker. I spent that day feeling a bit like a child trying to impress some grown-ups.

It is a long day, too. You're in the office in time to watch the early kick-off. Then you watch all of the 3 p.m. games, and then the Saturday evening one. By the time you go on air – live, once the news has finished – you've watched, assessed and analysed six hours of football. And then you have to condense each game down into about two minutes.

That time limit is what makes it so tough. Fans quite often complain that there isn't enough detail on *Match of the Day*, that we haven't taken enough things into account, or that we've only scratched the surface of the real story of the day. That's all you can do, though. After each game, you might have 50 seconds or a minute or so to identify and explain a single key point to the audience. That's it. There's no time to trip over your words or go into detail or have a discussion. There are no retakes, no second chances, no clever editing. It's all live, and you have to get everything you need to say into that one minute, or you've missed your chance. Everyone decides that you don't know what you're talking about and, thanks to the magic of social media, can let you know immediately.

Sky is a little different. On a Sunday, there is a little more time. You might have a couple of hours before a game, which is more than enough to shoehorn whatever point you want to make into a conversation. You still have to impress the collection of famous faces sitting around you, though, and when one of them is Roy Keane, that's easier said than done.

Before we started working together, I'd always wanted to meet Roy. Our paths never crossed as players. He left Manchester United before I started playing for Manchester City, so I never had the chance to dominate him in a derby. His reputation, though, goes before him. He won everything there is to win. He's a leader of men. He was a fearsome, relentless warrior. From what I'd seen of him on television, too, it was clear that he didn't suffer fools. He had no time for the nonsense that surrounds football. He spoke his mind. If you said something ridiculous, he'd fix you with that icy stare, the one that seems to go right through you, and put you back in your box. I knew that getting on his good side would be almost impossible, but I was desperate to quiz him. I wanted to see how he thought. I wanted to pick his brains. I wanted to find out if he was as intimidating, as serious, as angry as he seemed.

And then, not long after we'd started working together, I saw him sitting in a chair in a make-up room, staring into a mirror, delicately applying blusher to his own face. During the pandemic, Sky's Covid policy meant that we could no longer use make-up artists before going on air. Instead, they gave each of us our own toolkit, a little bag containing all of the things we'd need not to look like sweating gargoyles when we appeared on screen.

Now, to a young, dapper, well-groomed man like me, that's no bother at all. It's part and parcel of the job. You've got to look good. I don't mind making sure I catch the light in just the right way. But it was hard for me to square the public image of Roy – big beard, fierce eyes, endless disdain for anything showy or flashy or vain, a man who does not give the impression he cares what he looks like – with what I could see in the make-up room at Isleworth, which was a man in his mid-to-late forties making sure he'd got a nice, even coverage and a good, smooth finish. It was among the most ridiculous things I've ever seen. It is very hard to treat Roy Keane as the angriest man in football when you've seen him carefully powdering his forehead.

But then that image of Roy isn't quite right. He's not angry. He won't thank me for saying this, but secretly he's actually incredibly warm, and genuine, and kind. You might even describe him as nice, though you probably wouldn't say that to his face, no matter how much concealer he's wearing. He's the sort of person who hands you his phone number and insists – *insists* – that you get together for a drink the next time you're in his neck of the woods. 'Don't be leaving me out, now,' he said to me.

I'd be the first to admit that we have a bit of a weird dynamic. We shouldn't really get on. We're from opposite ends of the spectrum. I'm blue, he's red. I smile, he frowns. I laugh, he glares. I'm happy, he's always very cross. It might be that opposites attract, that it's our different approaches that let us play off each other. Or it might be that, deep down, Roy quite likes the fact that I'll give as good as I get.

I know, of course, that I don't have quite the same sort of authority as a lot of the other pundits in football. I haven't got quite as many medals as Roy or Thierry Henry.

I didn't captain England, like Gary Lineker. I haven't scored quite as many goals as Alan Shearer or Ian Wright. I didn't know David Beckham quite well, like Gary Neville.

But that doesn't mean that I can be dismissed. I'm happy to play the joker. I don't mind people treating me like the village idiot. But let's have this right: I've won the Premier League. I've played in the Champions League. I was the youngest defender ever to play for England. I might not have been quite as good as Roy Keane, but I wasn't too bad, you know. I've just always been aware, almost from that first moment when I messed up the joke about the pies, that if I wanted to make a career in broadcasting after football, then I couldn't just say the same things as everyone else. Nobody would take me seriously if I just parroted what Roy Keane had said, because his voice carries more weight. That meant I had to do things a little bit differently.

Sometimes, that means standing up to the others. It means telling Roy that I burst onto the scene, even if it is just a little self-deprecating, just to remind him that I might have just a little bit of an idea of what I'm talking about. Sometimes, it might mean reminding them that I'm quite a lot younger than they are, even if that means pointing out to Gary Lineker that all of his achievements came in black and white. Some pundits fall into the trap of analysing the game they see now as though it hasn't changed at all from the game they played then, when that couldn't be further from the truth. I am fresh out of it. I know what it is like to be a footballer now, and sometimes that needs to be expressed. That is what I think I bring to the table.

I don't like hearing players being accused of not caring enough. I don't like hearing that someone is too injury prone. I don't like hearing that such and such a player is only interested in the money. I know how much the players have to care to get to the point where people on television are picking holes in their performances. I know what it's like to get a lot of injuries, and I know that it's not a moral failing, a sign of weakness. I know that the money you get for being a player doesn't change how much you want to perform. Those are quite old-school views, and I'm not sure they really apply in the modern game. They don't feel like fair criticisms to me, and I'm happy to say so.

There are times, of course, when you do have to dig a player out, when you have to point to a mistake they've made, when you have to say something that might be difficult for them to hear. That can be awkward, but that is why you're there. That is your job. Most of the time, you know it's a mistake because you've made that error yourself. If I see a full-back being caught out at the far post, having been dragged too far inside, I'm happy to say what they've done wrong, but I'll make sure to mention that I've done that, too, a million times. I am young enough to remember what it is like to be in that position. I've always found that as long as you don't make it personal, players are understanding. They may not like it, but they accept that it's honest.

At that point, being relatively recently retired – and of the same generation as the players you're discussing – can be a weakness. Players do know what is being said about them. A lot of them will watch *Match of the Day*, or tune in to the live games on TV. Even if they don't, word gets back to them. They know who's got their back and who's on it.

It's something that can be hard to navigate. I've loved all of the chances I've had in the last few years to build my career in broadcasting, ever since the BBC and Sky first helped me on my way. I'm really grateful to Mark Chapman for encouraging me right at the start to do some work on Radio 5 Live, even though it means that I now tend to spend my Monday nights talking to Chris Sutton. The *Daily Mail* gave me the opportunity not just to write a column, but to sit down and interview some of my favourite people in football, too. I'm now one of the faces of the Champions League in the United States, thanks to CBS, and despite that, football keeps on getting more and more popular across the Atlantic.

That platform comes with responsibility, though. I've had players I've never met before message me out of the blue, asking me not to highlight their mistakes quite so much. It's never done particularly angrily, and there's never a row about it, but sometimes players feel that their errors are picked up on while others get away with it. Again, I've been there, too. Sometimes, players get in touch to thank you for not jumping on the bandwagon. A friend of mine was working with Paul Pogba before he left Manchester United, and he put him on the phone to me. I wasn't sure why, but he just wanted to say he appreciated me refusing to make him a scapegoat. At a time when he was really struggling for form, when he was the target of a lot of criticism from Manchester United fans, Harry Maguire texted me to say the same thing.

There are pundits who will protect their friends, not just by refusing to point out their errors but by encouraging others to leave them alone, too. There are even one or two who do a bit of work as agents, and are surprisingly positive about how their clients are doing. I don't have a relationship with people like Pogba or Maguire. I don't know them from Adam. I don't pull my punches because I'm worried they'll hear about it and get in touch. I don't take their side because I don't want to offend them.

I just try to be fair. That is the most important thing for any player who wants to get into broadcasting at the end of their career. If you can't swear live on the BBC as a teenager, and if you can't pick up loads of injuries so you have to retire when you should have been at your peak, it's best to make sure you treat everyone the same. There shouldn't be one rule for one player and another for everyone else, no matter how famous or beloved they are. That was all I'd ever asked for, during my career, and that's how I treat everyone now. That's the thing I try to remember. I've been there. I know how all of it feels.

16

WATER OFF A DUCK'S IMMACULATELY TAILORED BACK

I had a little ritual at the start of every game. Players all behave differently in those few minutes when you're waiting in the tunnel, lined up behind your captain, the opposition just a few feet away. Some like to have a chat. They might catch up with friends or former colleagues or international teammates, unless they're Frank Lampard. Some like to stare straight ahead. They won't meet your eye. They won't allow their focus to be broken. It's almost like they don't want to acknowledge their opponents are even there.

Neither of those quite worked for me. I liked to seek out whoever I would be up against that day. Playing at right-back isn't really about tactics or systems or playing philosophies. At heart, it's a one-on-one battle. It's you against the other guy. Whoever comes out on top is the one who gets to control the whole side of the pitch. I'd make a point of identifying my direct rival before the game and staring directly at them. Looking right into their eyes. I wanted to show them, whoever they were, that they weren't better than me. That I wasn't intimidated. I would know, from that point on, what sort of afternoon I was going to have. I knew if I had to be worried. I knew if I was going to dominate them.

I miss those moments. I miss having that fire in my belly. I miss the long, slow walk onto the pitch, the noise of the stadium going up a notch. I miss making that first tackle, crunching into an opponent. I miss hearing the roar that you get when you come out with the ball. I miss the fans singing my name. Or at least the possibility of the fans singing my name. Let's be honest, here: there aren't that many songs for the right-back. I miss playing big games. That's what I loved about football, really, even more than winning trophies. It was being involved in the games when everything was on the line. The now-or-never games.

Plenty of players struggle when they leave football, and we all have to leave football sooner or later, because football won't slow down for you, it won't wait. The biggest problem is always money. You get used to a certain sort of life as a player. So do your family. You think it's normal to change your car every six months, or every year, and to get the new one from a man you met in a hotel lobby. You think it's normal to have a £3 million mansion. You think it's normal that every little thing is done for you. You think it's normal to be able to call someone when the washing machine goes, and for them to sort out the person who comes to fix it. You think it's normal that all you need to pack when you go abroad is a little bag with some expensive aftershave in it, and maybe a bottle of ketchup. You think it's normal that you can't be trusted to look after your own passport.

That all goes away almost as soon as you retire. You might have built up a nice little fortune over the years, of course, but you can work your way through that pretty quickly when you don't have anything to do during the day. That money burns a hole in your pocket. Some players might have access to financial planners, but that's not the same as really understanding how to look after what you've earned. And most of the time there is nobody on hand to teach you the basics of how to look after yourself. It is getting better, but football does not do a good job of teaching players what life looks like after football. Managers and clubs only think about now, about what you can do right this minute, about the next game, about winning. Agents only think about what you can make at your peak. You're no use to them once you've stopped earning, once you've stopped bringing in deals, once you're no longer a hot property. You're cut loose and you're on your own.

Then there is the dressing room. That's something all players find it difficult to replace. The dressing room, in a lot of ways, isn't a healthy environment. It is unforgiving. It looks for any form of weakness and exploits it ruthlessly. It is not understanding or forgiving or patient. Football is dog eat dog. But it is also the only place you've ever known. The noise, the banter, the feeling of being part of something bigger than you: it's what you've been used to your whole life. You notice it when it's gone.

I would miss it, too, if working in the media wasn't at least a little bit similar. I spend most of my time now in studios, whether it's a big game on Sky, covering the

Champions League for the American network CBS, arguing with Chris Sutton on the *Monday Night Club* on 5 Live or breaking down an entire day's action for *Match of the Day*. All of the players I come across still have a little bit of the dressing room in them. Spending eight hours in a small room with Alan Shearer and Ian Wright or Roy Keane and Jamie Carragher is just as fun and just as merciless as being in among your teammates. I can't miss the dressing room because most of the time it feels like I'm still there. We're all just scrubbed up nice, rather than wearing training gear, and the fines system isn't quite as strict.

What I don't miss, not in the slightest, is all of the stuff that goes along with football. It was difficult enough when I was playing, and all we had to deal with, really, was the press. I had to get used to seeing my performances criticised. I never minded that, particularly. That's the job. Everyone is going to have an opinion. And if you've played badly, you don't need to be told. You'll know. And if you weren't sure, your teammates won't waste any time in telling you. Most players are fine with that. As long as the criticism isn't personal, as long as you're not saying I've played badly because of the type of person I am, or because I'm doing this thing off the field, then that's not a problem.

From the outside, it looks a thousand times worse to me now. I made my debut before Twitter even existed. I think I'd joined it and left again because of the abuse before some clubs had even worked out what it was. It was only as I was playing that it started to become more relevant, and it was never as dominant as it is now. I see some of the stuff that players have to deal with now and I genuinely don't know if I'd have been able to handle it: all of that poison coming at you constantly, through your phone. I look at the treatment someone like Harry Maguire has had and it disgusts me.

Then there are the cameraphones. We had to deal with paparazzi, obviously. We knew that there was a certain spot on the path around Manchester City's old training ground where they used to hang out, where they could get a shot of everything that was happening on the training pitch. Or at least there was, until Roberto Mancini had a fence put up to stop them. We knew that if we had a fight in training then there was a pretty good chance it would end up in the papers the next day. (Just like the fines, it didn't always prove a deterrent.) We knew that we had to leave nightclubs by the back door if we wanted to go unnoticed. We knew that if we wanted to have our photo taken – though I'm not sure why we would have done that – there were ways of making sure the photographers just happened to be in the right place at the right time.

But we didn't have to deal with cameraphones, not at the start, anyway, not when I was dipping my toe in Manchester's social scene. Everyone in the club wasn't a potential paparazzo. It was all Nokia 3210s and those thin Motorola ones. I can't say for certain if I'd have been allowed to become a footballer if I'd come through now. I would have been in the papers every single week for being out and about. I'd have been caught breaking curfew dozens of times. I'd have contributed as much to the fine pot as Balotelli. The club wouldn't have thought I was worth the trouble. As it was, I had chance to be young, and to make mistakes without all of them appearing online within 24 hours. I don't know if players get that anymore. Maybe they've just got really good at moving silently. Maybe they're all as good as David Silva used to be.

I don't miss any of that, all of the stuff that surrounds football, football as an industry. I don't miss the perception of footballers. Some jobs are more than just jobs. They're stereotypes. Estate agent. Journalist. Geography teacher. It's the same for footballers. That word creates an image for people. Footballers are flash, and stupid, and ungrateful. They're arrogant and spoiled. That's true of some of them, obviously. It's not true of all of us, just as it's not true that all estate agents are shifty, all journalists are sly, and all geography teachers are nerds. But that is how people see you: as a footballer, and that word conjures up certain feelings.

Mostly, they have to do with money. It is why whenever you hear players talk about things like depression or stress there is always someone shutting them down. How can someone with that much money be depressed? The fact that they have a nice house and a flash car has nothing to do with their mental health, of course, but that doesn't seem to matter. People hear 'footballer' and they think money.

Footballers do earn ridiculous amounts, of course they do. They do sometimes spend it on stupid things. They do make themselves an easy target. But they are also scapegoats. They're a punching bag. It's easy to have a go at these young men who have all the money in the world just because they're good at kicking a ball around. They're a way for people to take out their frustrations about the rest of society. But the money isn't the fault of the players. They didn't make the industry go the way it has. Throughout my career, I never met a player who was solely motivated by money. Agents, yes. I met plenty of agents who thought about nothing else. And I met plenty of players who enjoyed spending it, and who would happily move clubs if they didn't feel they were getting paid enough of it. But there isn't a single player out there who got involved in football because they wanted to make money. Nobody woke up as a kid and thought that was the career for them because it was a good way to get rich.

Maybe their parents did. Maybe their parents wanted their child to be a Premier League footballer because it would set them up for life. But not the players. The players don't play for money. They play because they love playing football. They spend all of those hours driving to training sessions, listening to their dads tell them about puberty, because they love football. They put up with being berated by senior players because they love playing football. They deal with managers banning the colour purple and screaming instructions at them for 90 minutes because they love playing football. They tell a doctor to drain the fluid from their knee just one more time because they love playing football.

It was that perception that I found hardest to deal with during my career, the idea that people saw me in a certain way just because of the job I did. People assumed they knew what I was like, they knew what made me tick, even if they'd never met me. I found that personal criticism difficult.

Now, I am much better equipped to handle it. If people want to tell me I'm a bad pundit, that I don't know what I'm talking about, if they want to have a go at me on social media, that's fine. It's water off a duck's back. But that is only because of everything I went through as a player. You have to learn to be resilient as a player. I know, now, that nothing can ever be as bad as what I went through at the lowest point of my career, those last two years at Aston Villa. That was the end of me as a footballer, but I look back on it as the making of me as a person. If I made it through that and came out the other side, then there isn't much that can faze me.

It's that, more than anything, that has allowed me to have a second life, a second career. Part of the reason that I don't miss football is because I still feel like I'm part of it. I know how lucky I am to have that chance, to be able to sit around in a nice suit talking about the thing I love, occasionally stopping to call Gary Lineker old or Alan Shearer bald or to wind Roy Keane up and watch him go. Not everyone gets the chance to burst onto two scenes, after all. I'm even luckier that I can do it by being myself. I don't have to worry about playing to the crowd or being controversial for the sake of it. I can do it the way I want to do it safe in the knowledge that I don't mind what people say about me. I can show them who I really am, not who they might think I am because of the job I did.

There is part of me that knows, had things been different, that I could still be playing. Give me a better pair of knees and I would still be out there. There are a couple of current defences that would definitely benefit from a fully fit Micah Richards. I would have aged gracefully into a ball-playing centre-back, I think, spraying passes around from deep, blaming the full-backs when things went wrong. I would love to still be playing, of course I would. I would play for free if my body was up to it.

But while I regret the way my career ended, I don't regret the fact that it has. I never look back and feel sorry for myself that I played my last game when I was 28. I never worry that something that started so brightly lasted so briefly. I like to think that I packed plenty into those ten years. I saw everything football has to offer, all of its sides and its faces, its highs and its lows, and, thanks to Mario Balotelli, pretty much all of the strangeness in between. I learned everything there is to know about the game. And while I might not have been invincible, at least I can say I survived.

ACKNOWLEDGEMENTS

I've really enjoyed taking the time to look back on my career, and it's clear to me I owe a fair few thank-yous, so here goes.

I owe a huge debt to two school teachers who went the extra mile to help me as an aspiring footballer. Mr Moore at Archbishop Cranmer Primary School, who got me my first trials, and Mr King from Wetherby High, who would often take me to training when my dad wasn't able to. Such was Mr King's influence, he was the first person I rang when I got a senior England call-up. I must also mention Paul and Kath Priest, who looked after me like a son in my Manchester digs.

Manchester City will always hold a huge place in my heart and there are some wonderful people at the club. In particular, Brandon Ashton and Les 'Chappy' Chapman are the two most likeable kit men you could ever hope to meet and played a huge part in the special atmosphere at the club. Karen Procter, now Head of Protocol and Player Activation, has been with the club over 15 years and can never do enough for me. Vicky Kloss headed up Communications at the club for over 20 years until this summer and is a talented and special lady. A note of appreciation too for Khaldoon al-Mubarak, the club's CEO, who has always treated me extremely well, as has Brian Marwood, Managing Director of City Football Group.

Given my injury record, it's no surprise I named in this book many members of the Manchester City medical department whom I owe thanks to, but additionally I'd like to recognise the role of Dr Ricky Shamji and Jon Hartley when I was at Aston Villa, in what was a really difficult period for me.

I was fortunate to have some great teammates who have become close friends, none more so than Joe Hart, Joleon Lescott and Daniel Sturridge. I'll always value our friendships.

I want to also acknowledge my accountant Chris Farthing, whom I've known since I was 17. He has always been the person I can most trust. Thanks also to James Black, my agent for the final stages of my playing career, who remains a very close friend. I must also thank my friend Maj Khadim, who did more than anyone else to help me when I felt at my lowest during a dark period as my career came to an end.

As you'll have now read, I certainly wasn't sure I'd move into the media, but if there's one colleague who deserves a special mention then it's Mark Chapman. He couldn't have done more to help me transition from footballer to pundit, and he remains hugely encouraging.

ACKNOWLEDGEMENTS

Going behind the camera, I'm indebted to Steve Rudge, Head of Football at the BBC, alongside his colleagues Ben North, Steve Houghton and Richard Hughes for their support. It would be remiss not to acknowledge Rob Nothman and Matt Curtis for their training and advice, or Dominic King at the *Daily Mail* for his guidance with my column.

I'm fortunate also to work with Sky Sports, and in that respect I owe thanks to Gary Hughes and Adam Craig. Thanks also to Matt Roberts, Billy McGinty and Jack Hazzard – all talented producers who have helped my development. I must mention Pete Radovich at CBS Sports, who has made me a key part of his team, broadcasting the Champions League to the USA. I feel lucky to work alongside the very best pundits and broadcasters, and I'd like to thank all of my colleagues.

Thanks also to Josh Landy and Eli Wegrzyn at Bear Faced Talent for all your support in my second career, and to Rory Smith for helping me tell this story, as well as Oliver Malcolm and his team at HarperCollins.

Finally, and most importantly – thank you to Mum and Dad. You both made sacrifices for all your children and, in particular, you gave me the best chance of making it as a professional footballer. Words aren't enough to show my gratitude.

PICTURE CREDITS